A GREAT WEEKEND IN

LONDON

A GREAT WEEKEND IN LONDON

Who could resist the special appeal of London? The great British capital is very easy to get to, wherever you're starting from, and it really does have something for everyone. You can still find the London of formal elegance, cosy tradition and pageantry, but it's also a dynamic city, pumped up with youthful energy, at the cutting edge of creativity. London leads the way with the most outrageous fashions and its wild night clubs are the envy of the world.

You may be looking for high quality cashmere, a classic raincoat or a pair of stack-heeled, sequin-spangled shoes. You may be dreaming of royal pomp and circumstance or itching to get down on the dance floor of the world's hottest clubs. Whatever you're looking for, look no further! London has everything you want.

This city is the shop window of the western world. Its large stores and little shops are filled with goods of all kinds to suit every taste and budget. Its many different ethnic communities have further enriched London's vast warehouse with their own particular contributions, and in a couple of hours your shopping expedition can take you right round the world.

With its six million inhabitants and wide area, London is all

things to all people: from the Sloane Ranger to the 'lovable Cockney'. Neighbourhoods have been enhanced by newcomers from the Caribbean, Africa and the Indian subcontinent. The city has its own unique street poetry. Here the majestic clouds of Turner's paintings reflect in the puddles on the pavement, and round the next corner a turbanned Sikh and the smell of spices will transport you briefly to Bombay, even though you've just come out of Marks and Spencer's. You may be passed by a girl with one side of her head shaven and the other sprouting pink hair, a covey of sharply-dressed City boys in three-piece suits with mobile phones clamped to their ears, a gaggle of Chinese shopkeepers from Soho, a Margaret Rutherford type in a twin-set, a Rasta with dreadlocks or a West End lady, with shoes in hand,

revelling in the feel of the Hyde Park grass beneath her feet. Styles and looks of every kind rub shoulders with each other, arousing the most supreme indifference. No one passes judgement or expresses surprise. It's only the tourists who turn their heads to watch a shaven-headed couple walk by with their noses and lips pierced. Perhaps Londoners owe this independent spirit and indifference to appearances to the fact

that, far from being slaves to fashion, they create it themselves, new every day. Their fantastic inventions, a combination of junk, imagination and resourcefulness, are now copied on fashion catwalks throughout the world. London's creative dynamism comes from an independence of mind and spirit and continual absorbtion of new ideas from every corner of the earth. Like some distant planet where misery has been banished, this city is the best possible destination to raise your spirits. So forget your problems, drop all inhibitions and revel in the eccentricity. You're in London and you'll be amazed at how free it makes you feel. After cramming every moment of your weekend with activities, you'll leave vowing to be back, very soon.

How to get there

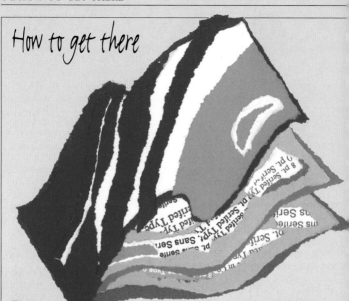

PICK YOUR MOMENT

WHAT TO DO

There's enough to do in London to fill a year of weekends. But the capital has so many special events throughout the year – the Boat Show, the Ideal Home Exhibition, art exhibitions, West End shows, Buckingham Palace, the Millennium Dome, Wimbledon and the Chelsea Flower Show– that you might want to pick the time of your visit to coincide with a particular occasion.

HOW TO GET THERE

FROM WITHIN THE UK

If you're starting off from somewhere in the UK, then the plane or the train can take the strain, or there are coaches from hundreds of towns across the country which bring you into Victoria Coach station. Don't even try to bring a car into Central London – the roads are busy and the parking, if you can find a space, is exorbitant.

BY TRAIN

Trains come into the mainline stations from all major and many smaller cities and towns in the the country. For information about the services run by the train companies, call the UK train enquiry number ☎ 0345 484950. Check out what Saver deals are available when you call.

BY COACH

Getting to London is often a good deal cheaper by coach than by train. National Express Coaches reservations are on ☎ 08705 808080 or 0990 808080. They also have an on-line booking service on their website at www.nationalexpress.co.uk Here you can find details of the trips they organise to events such as the Boat Show, the Ideal Home Exhibition or the Millennium Dome. Coaches come into Victoria Coach Station. There's also a reservation service there on ☎ 020 7730 3499.

BY PLANE

London has five airports but there's no hassle-free way of getting into town. **Heathrow Airport** (☎ 0870 0000123) is the closest, 15 miles out, and there's a choice of ways of getting into the city. You can catch an Airport Bus (☎ 0990 747777). The A1 goes direct to Victoria Station or the A2 goes to King's Cross station, stopping at Notting Hill, Baker Street and Euston Station. A single ticket costs £7, or £12 for a return. The Underground (Piccadilly Line) costs £3.50 one-way, and has regular trains from all terminals from 4.58am in the week or 5.47am on Sundays. The journey lasts about 50 minutes. Trains on this line stop at Piccadilly Circus, Leicester Square and Covent Garden.

The fastest way of getting into the centre of London is by the Heathrow Express train to Paddington Station, (☎ 0845 6001515), £12 single or £22 return. The journey takes only 15 minutes. and trains leave every 15 minutes. The first train leaves Heathrow at 5.10am and the last train at 11.40pm. The most expensive way is to take a taxi which could cost as much as £30.

From **Gatwick Airport**, take the 30-minute ride on the Gatwick Express train into Victoria Station. Trains leave every 15 minutes and a single fare costs £10.20.

London's **City Airport**, (☎ 020 7646 0000) in the old port area of the city, is served by the Dockland's Light Railway, which also goes to the Millennium Dome.

From **Luton Airport**, (☎ 01582 410100), you can take a Greenline coach, £7.20 single or £11.80 return,

SALES

The main sales periods for London stores are January-February and June-July. Get there early because they are very popular, particularly sales in the large stores, which offer major price reductions. However an increasing number of shops now run promotions all year round, in which the prices of some items are lowered by varying amounts.

which takes 30 minutes to get to Victoria Coach Station, or, more comfortable but more of a hassle, take the shuttle bus to Luton Station for the regular train services, £9.20 single or £16.90 return, to King's Cross Station.

From **Stansted Airport**, (☎ 01279 680 500), the so-called Skytrain, £12 single to Liverpool Street Station, takes 45 minutes, and the trains run every 15 minutes.

Lots of airlines offer flights into the five different London airports.

British Airways, ☎ 020 7434 4700 or on-line at www.british-airways.com, flies from Dublin, Cork, Belfast, Glasgow, Edinburgh, Inverness, Manchester, Sheffield (into City Airport) and Newcastle.

British Midland, ☎ 0870 607055 or on-line bookings at www.britishmidland.co.uk, flies from Dublin, Belfast, Edinburgh and Glasgow.

Aer Lingus and Ryan Air fly from Dublin and Easy-Jet from Liverpool, Edinburgh, Glasgow, and Aberdeen into Luton. Jersey European Airlines have services from Belfast to Luton or Dublin to City Airport, where Scotair also flies out of Dunfermline, Edinburgh and Glasgow.

EMBASSIES AND HIGH COMMISSIONS

If you're in London from overseas and have a serious problem, your Embassy or High Commission can provide assistance. They're all located in the centre of London.

Australian High Commission, Australia House, Strand, WC2
☎ 020 7379 4344
⊖ Temple

New Zealand High Commission, New Zealand House, 80 Haymarket, SW1
☎ 020 7930 8422
⊖ Piccadilly Circus

High Commission of the Republic of South Africa South Africa House Trafalgar Square, WC2
☎ 020 7451 7299
⊖ Charing Cross or Leicester Square

Irish Embassy
17 Grosvenor Place, SW1
☎ 020 7235 2171
Fax 020 7245 6961

Canadian High Commission MacDonald House
1 Grosvenor Square, W1
☎ 020 7258 6600
⊖ Bond Street

United States Embassy
24 Grosvenor Square, W1
☎ 020 7499 9000
⊖ Bond Street

FROM THE USA AND CANADA

If you're flying from the US., British Airways, American Airlines (www.aa.com) or United, (www.united-airlines.com) have shoals of flights from the major American airports – New York, Washingdon DC, Miami, Chicago, Atlanta, Dallas, Seattle, Los Angeles and San Francisco. Flying on Air Canada, the national carrier, there are direct flights from airports across the country. For flight information or reservations, call
☎ 01888 247 2262.

FROM AUSTRALIA AND NEW ZEALAND

Qantas (www.webjet.com.au) and Air New Zealand (www.airnz.com) both offer on-line booking facilities for flights to the UK.

HIRING A CAR

There's really no point hiring a car if you're only in London for the weekend. Not that anyone used to driving on the right need have any fears, particularly as directions and traffic instructions are generally clearly signposted, but you'll spend a fortune on parking and waste an awful lot of time looking for a space, particularly in the main shopping areas, or sitting in the legendary traffic jams. There are a great many pedestrianised areas in London, and the public transport, both buses and the underground rail network or 'tube', is very efficient. For those driving fanatics who can't bear to be without their own set of wheels, cars can

be hired from a company such as Jet Tours, as long as you've held a driving licence for at least three years.

ENTRY FORMALITIES

If you're coming to London from outside the UK and are a citizen of a member state of the European Union, all you need to enter the country is an identity card or valid passport. Coming from Australia or New Zealand, there are various limits to the time visitors are entitled to stay, especially when coming to work. To avoid problems at the port of entry, check with the British consulate or High Commission before you leave home. Coming from North America, no visas are required, but you must have a valid passport.

CUSTOMS

Don't forget that it's illegal to bring animals into Britain. All pets that are brought into Britain will be confined to a six-month quarantine on arrival to make sure rabies isn't brought into the country. Don't try to get round this law, as you could end up spending two days in prison and paying a hefty fine.

You're allowed to bring 200 cigarettes into the country if you've bought them duty free, and 800 if they were bought in a member country of the European Union. Determined smokers may prefer to bring their favourite brand with them, as tobacco is very expensive in the UK.

Where alcohol is concerned, the duty free limit is 1 litre for alcoholic drinks over 22°, 2 litres at less than 22° or 2 bottles of wine. Ten times this limit is allowed for products bought in France. You can also buy 2.5 litres of eau de Cologne or 60 cl of perfume duty free. There's no ceiling on goods purchased within the European Union.

Importing meat, milk, eggs and more than 2kg/4lbs 6oz of fruit and vegetables is strictly forbidden.

You should certainly not try to bring any defensive weapon, such as a teargas spray, into the country. If you do so, you risk a heavy fine. Almost all such weapons are illegal in the UK, with alarm systems only being permitted.

INSURANCE

It's advisable to take out insurance to cover the cost of repatriation in case of a serious accident. Travel agents

usually offer this type of insurance or can include it as part of your package. In addition, you can also get cover if using your credit card to pay for your booking.

CURRENCY AND BUDGETING

The British currency is the pound sterling (£), which divides into 100 pence (p). It comes in notes with a value of £5, £10, £20, £50, or more, and coins of £2 or £1 and 1, 2, 5, 10, 20 or 50 pence. If you are coming from overseas, it's better to change your money at home as most British banks are closed at the weekend, though some open on Saturday mornings. Bureaux de Change generally offer poor rates.

Whatever you do, make sure you have a minimum amount of English currency when you arrive at the airport or station, at least enough to pay for your transfer to the hotel. That way, you won't have to waste time standing in a long queue for the Bureau de Change. You'll find automatic cash dispensers everywhere, though, and you can use your credit card to withdraw cash from these instantly. If you want to take a large sum with you, take it in traveller's cheques, which are more secure. To avoid paying too much commission, buy them in large units and try to change them at a branch of the issuing bank.

HEALTH

If you're having medical treatment, bring a full course of drugs with you. Prescription drugs can't be bought over the counter in the UK.

The ambulance, police and fire are all on the same telephone number, ☎ **999**. Use this number only in life-threatening situations. London hospitals are overworked, so use their accident and emergency services only in cases of serious need. If you need advice, go to a pharmacy. Some stay open late.

Zafash Pharmacy (24 hrs)
233-235 Old Brompton Rd, SW5
☎ 020 7373 2798
⊖ Earls Court Rd

Bliss Chemists (9am–midnight)
5-6 Marble Arch, W1
☎ 020 7373 2798
⊖ Marble Arch

Boots (9am–8pm)
Piccadilly Circus, W1
☎ 020 7734 6126
⊖ Piccadilly Circus

LOCAL TIME

In winter, the UK follows Greenwich Mean Time, GMT, the time at London's famous Greenwich meridian, marked on the ground in the Old Royal Observatory courtyard. GMT runs from the last Sunday in October to the last Sunday in March, when the clocks move forward one hour ahead of GMT, to British Summer Time. BST runs from the last Sunday in March to the last Sunday in October. Wellington, New Zealand, is 12 hours ahead of GMT, Sydney, Australia, is 10 hours ahead, while New York and Toronto are 5 hours behind GMT and Los Angeles is 8 hours behind. If you need to check local time while you're in London, you can telephone the Speaking Clock ☎123.

VOLTAGE

The standard UK current is 240 volts. If the voltage at home is different from this, you won't be able to use your appliances in London unless you either take an adaptor or buy one at the airport. Otherwise you'll have to leave the electric razor and hairdryer at the bottom of your suitcase.

SURVIVAL KIT

To find out how to get around in London, first purchase an A-Z map of the city and an Underground (tube) map. Equipped with these, you'll be able to orientate yourself and find locations off the map on pp. 78-79.

The best way of finding out what's on in London

USEFUL ADDRESSES

For a selection of brochures and guides to many of the sights in London, details of tours and shopping, and up-to-date information about events, visit one of the tourist information centres. They also sell a good range of visitor publications. London Tourist Board runs pre-recorded information lines including; accommodation ☎ 0891 505 487; events ☎ 0839 123 4000 and children's activities ☎ 0839 123 404.

London Tourist Board Information Centre
Victoria Station Forecourt, SW1 (no telephone)
Open daily 8am–7pm.● Victoria

Britain Visitor Centre
1 Regent Street, W1 (no telephone)
Open Mon-Fri 9am–6.30pm, Sat-Sun 10am–4pm.
● Piccadilly

City of London Tourist Information
St. Paul's Churchyard, EC4 ☎ 020 7332 1456
Open 1 April–1 October daily 9am–5pm then
Mon-Fri 9am-5pm, Sat 9.30am–12.30. ● St. Paul's

GUIDED TOURS

The easy way to see London is on the top deck of a double-decker bus or from a river boat on the Thames. London also has a network of canals, and from the vantage point on a barge, you get an entirely different picture of the city.

Big Bus Company (☎ 020 8944 7810) or the **Original London Sightseeing Bus** (☎ 020 8877 1722), operate tours round the capital. Hop on anywhere and hop off when you want to look at a monument up close.

Westminster Passenger Service (☎ 020 7930 4097) go down the Thames from Westminster pier, or **Jenny Wren** (☎ 020 7485 4433) operate canal cruises from Camden Lock.

during your stay is to buy a copy of the Evening Standard, London's evening newspaper, or Time Out, a weekly listings magazine.

If you lose something while travelling around London, report your loss to a police station and call the lost property offices:
Tube ☎ 020 7486 2496
Bus ☎ 020 7222 1234
Taxi ☎ 020 7833 0996

THE CROWN JEWELS

Since the Civil war of 1649 and the restoration of the monarchy in 1660, British monarchs have gradually ceded power. The United Kingdom is a parliamentary democracy and the sovereign has no political power. However the monarch is Head of State and fulfils a constitutional role in ceremonies of great pageantry, such as the State Opening of Parliament.

THE CROWN UNDER THREAT

Much has gone wrong for the Windsors. Although there have been countless revelations about royal doings in books, on television and in the papers, the tragic death of Princess Diana posed the greatest challenge ever to the very existence of the monarchy. Since the bitter speech made at Diana's funeral by her brother Lord Spencer, the Royal Family's advisers have been struggling to polish up the crown's image. They are the source of endless fascination and the tabloid newspapers pursue their Royal prey, taking cruel delight in the family's misfortunes. The best-known of these, *The Sun* (circulation 4 million) has played its own part in tarnishing the royal family's image.

ROYAL FORTUNES AND MISFORTUNES

As proud possessor of the world's three largest diamonds, two-thirds of all the known drawings by Leonardo da Vinci and a fortune estimated at £3 billion, Queen Elizabeth is not about to be put out on the street. But things have changed. Since April 1994, the queen pays income tax just like her subjects. The civil list, the public money allocated to her and her immediate family by Parliament, represents

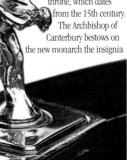

only 32 pence per person. However more and more of the British people now think this is too much: over 50% of them predict that the monarchy will not survive beyond the 2050s.

GOD SAVE THE QUEEN !

Since 1066 the stages of the sovereign's life have been marked in Westminster Abbey. At the coronation, the monarch enters the Abbey and sits on Edward the Confessor's throne, which dates from the 15th century. The Archbishop of Canterbury bestows on the new monarch the insignia

THE CEREMONY OF THE KEYS

To watch the Ceremony of the Keys at first hand, you can buy a ticket from the Tower of London on the day. However, if you don't manage to get a ticket, you can simply watch from outside. At exactly 9.53pm, the Chief Yeoman Warder and his escort, dressed in black and scarlet Tudor costumes and holding lanterns, come to shut the outer gate. They then close all the other gates of the Tower in turn. The keys are saluted by the sentinels as they pass and the Chief Warder ends with the traditional three cheers for the Queen. This ritual, which is nearly seven centuries old, lasts only seven minutes, but you'll be observing at first hand one of the traditions to which the British give such weight and importance. This ceremony is attended by comparatively few people, particularly when it's performed after dark, so it's far more intimate and mysterious than the changing of the guard with its throngs of tourists.

largest diamonds in the world (the Star of Africa), the orb surmounted by a cross, symbolising the power of Christ on earth, and the sovereign's ring of sapphires and rubies, decorated with the English emblem of the cross of St George. All these insignia represent the monarch's role as Head of State and and also as Head of the Anglican Church. You can see them all at the Tower of London (see p. 60). The coronation of Elizabeth II in 1953 was the first royal ceremony to be broadcast live on television, making history in more ways than one.

THE CHANGING OF THE GUARD

The changing of the guard at Buckingham Palace opens with a fanfare. It takes place daily at

11.30am from April to September, and every other day from October to March, unless it's raining. There are often big crowds which means that you might not get a very good view, so try going to the Horse Guards building on Whitehall, where exactly the same ceremony takes place at 11am on weekdays and 10am on Sundays and the crowds are much smaller.

of power: the sword, the mantle, the crown, the sceptre, which is set with one of the

INTO THE NEW MILLENNIUM

Of all the European capitals, London certainly displays the greatest creative dynamism. Most of the late 20th-century trends started here and that driving force can be felt in fashion, music, art, design and, above all, on the street. In London, you can see the avant garde re-inventing itself before your very eyes and glimpse trends that will catch on elsewhere maybe months or even years later.

VIVIENNE WESTWOOD: FROM AVANT-GARDE SHOCKER TO MAINSTREAM

This co-founder of the Punk movement started out designing clothes for the Sex Pistols before becoming one of Britain's most notorious fashion designers. Today you'll find the most elegant women fighting over her eccentric creations, including long-line strapless bras and jackets. Although she's become something of an institution these days and her designs are increasingly regarded as good taste, they're still full of challenging inventiveness and creativity.

DESIGNERS FOR FASHION VICTIMS

The widest possible variety of styles coexist in London, from the most classic to the most outrageous. You'll find an amazing degree of sartorial licence in the street. London's eccentricity is fostered by a posse of newly-established designers, such as Julien MacDonald and Hussein Chalayan, and big names such as Tomasz Starzeweski and John Galliano.

THE CRUCIBLE OF MODERN ARCHITECTURE

The vast Docklands regeneration scheme, east of the City, was intended to create a new financial district to challenge the Square Mile. Through the recession of the early 1990s, offices in many of the striking buildings remained vacant, but with the surge of economic recovery Docklands has become more lively and energetic, attracting an increasing number of artists.

TRIUMPHANT TECHNO

Techno, a musical genre that first appeared in 1989, has been triumphantly successful in London. Every weekend, world-famous DJs play their music in the city's multitude of clubs, including the famous Ministry of Sound (see p. 121).

CELEBRATING 2000

To celebrate the year 2000, a gigantic dome has been built at Greenwich. Its cost is put at £750 million, and the whole project has been highly controversial. Inside there are fourteen 'zones' to visit, mapping life, work, religion and science in 'Cool Britannia'. Another dramatic construction is the London Eye, an observation wheel towering 135m (440ft) above the South Bank and offering panoramic views of London.

GRAPHICS AND NEW MAGAZINES

The British advertising industry and press regularly win international prizes and are currently world leaders. Just look at the ads on the tube or flick through some of the magazines – the ones with the biggest following include *ID*, *Dazed and Confused*, *The Face* and the very arty *Frieze*.

GADGETS FOR TOMORROW

The Design museum is the first museum devoted entirely to industrial design. British design is highly original and by no means limited to luxury products, and

is often at its most expressive in everyday objects, which makes it very affordable too. Look for designs by Ron Arad, for example.

A DYNAMIC ART SCENE

Since the emergence of what's been called 'the new British

sculpture' in the early 1980s, the London art scene has gone from strength to strength. This is as true of the galleries

LITTLE HOLES, AND MORE LITTLE HOLES...

Any part of your body, from your nose to your eyebrows, navel, lips, tongue and more uncomfortable places, can be pierced with a ring, bar or stud. Body piercing has replaced tattooing among the more eccentric and less squeamish of London's youth. It started with the hippest and trendiest but is now so widespread that all kinds of people in almost all walks of life pierce their bodies with odd bits of metal.

and museums as it is of the alternative (non-commercial) venues. The turbulent Damien Hirst, of pickled sheep fame, maker of videos and winner of the 1995 Turner Prize, has almost become mainstream.

LONDON IN THE LATE BAROQUE PERIOD

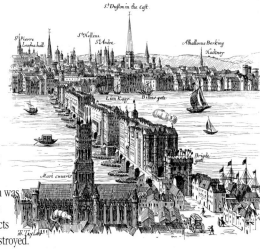

The plague and the Great Fire of London were the most devastating events of the time. Much of London had to be rebuilt, and the architect Sir Christopher Wren was commissioned to rebuild the districts that had been destroyed. He designed some hundred churches in the City many of which can still be seen today, the greatest being the famous St Paul's Cathedral.

POLITICAL UPHEAVALS

The great changes in the capital's layout took place during a turning point in the country's history. Over the period between 1642, when Charles I was beheaded and Cromwell, the Lord Protector, came to power, and 1688, when William of Orange came to the throne, a parliamentary democracy developed that became the model for Europe in the Age of Enlightenment. It was a time of economic dynamism when the middle classes enjoyed great prosperity and the capital city spread.

MEDIEVAL PLANNING AND PREHISTORIC HYGIENE

The growth of the city was anarchic and based on methods from the Middle Ages. The houses were all built of wood and packed together in very narrow streets, which greatly increased the fire hazard. These dwellings were often seriously overcrowded, with

The Monument in the City commemorates the Great Fire.

poor ventilation and almost no form of sanitation. In such insanitary conditions, disease inevitably spread. The Great Plague of 1665 claimed nearly 70,000 lives.

EVERY CLOUD HAS A SILVER LINING...

It never rains but it pours... The following year, in 1666, the Great Fire of London raged unchecked for five days and nights, consuming the city's narrow streets and laying waste to 13,000 houses and 89 churches, in other words almost all of London's old centre. The ravaged site more or less corresponds to

LONDON IN THE LATE BAROQUE PERIOD ■ 15

the area that makes up the City of London. It's thought that the fire started in a baker's shop, but at the time rumours abounded that it was all part of a Papist plot. This belief was so firmly held by some that reprisals were taken against Catholics. The fire destroyed the insanitary city and cleansed it of the plague.

SIR CHRISTOPHER WREN (1632-1723)

There was no special reason why Christopher Wren should have been chosen to rebuild London after the Great Fire. He had had no more than the standard education received by an educated man of his time, consisting mainly of mathematics and medicine. However, he held the position of chief architect to Charles II, who was then on the throne, and so the king gave him the job. Wren was an ambitious visionary, who wanted to redesign the entire city, giving it broad avenues leading to monumental squares. However these plans proved too expensive and were abandoned.

REBUILDING FROM SCRATCH

The fact that reconstructing the city necessarily involved starting from scratch made it possible to establish new municipal regulations for the work of rebuilding. For example, the Building Act of 1667 set the minimum width for streets at 5.5m/6yd and banned building houses in wood, which was replaced by brick. However, these measures did not constitute a truly coherent rebuilding plan and construction work was no sooner finished than the district was abandoned by the aristocracy, who moved to the western suburbs, known as the West End. The new City was rebuilt on the old medieval layout and today's taxi drivers no doubt regret that Sir Christopher Wren wasn't given the means to design a city along his visionary lines.

KEEP CLEAR TURNING BAY

DONT EVEN THINK OF PARKING HERE

THE CITY'S CHURCHES

It was in the City, around the new St Paul's Cathedral (see p. 60), that architect Sir Christopher Wren created the greatest number of churches. Most of them are built of pale Portland stone, which is a strong contrast to the colourful red brick of the neighbouring buildings. Wren was highly imaginative and inventive, using a wide range of designs and often drawing on Roman models. The works were extremely expensive, and a new tax on coal was introduced to fund the rebuilding.

St Paul's Cathedral, 18th-century engraving.

DEDICATED FOLLOWERS OF BEAU BRUMMELL

Lord Brummell was a famous 19th-century dandy. As the leader of style and elegance of the day, he has left his mark on London fashion. Although bespoke tailors' prices are every bit as high as their reputations might suggest, you'll find that luxury and quality go hand in hand. There are a great many excellent shops, and you're bound to come across at least one of them during the course of your stay.

BARBOUR JACKETS: OFF-THE-PEG OILCLOTH

The reputation of these waxed cotton jackets has stood since 1890. They were originally worn as hunting clothes because the water-proofing was high quality, but their chic-yet-relaxed look means they make a great replacement for the more traditional mac when worn over a suit, for example. Barbour jackets are usually three-quarter length and the most common colour is spruce green with a brown corduroy collar; some also have a removable lining. To ensure your jacket will last, it should be waxed once a year with a product you can usually buy at the same time as the jacket.

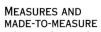

MEASURES AND MADE-TO-MEASURE

Tailors in London aren't the kind to go in for double standards, but they're usually more than happy to provide half-measures:

once you've selected the body you want for your shirt from the standard models on offer, the collar and sleeves will be made to fit your measurements. Next you must select your fabric. Silky 'sea island' cotton, with its extra long fibres, is the finest and smartest. Sober poplin is best for classic-style shirts, while the thickness of Oxford makes it better suited to garments with a more casual look.

TRENCH COATS: GENTRIFIED MILITARY COATS

'Trench coats' were originally designed during the First World War to be worn by British soldiers in the bitter cold of the Verdun battlefield. They're still very popular, and the name has entered everyday language. They've now become a bone of contention between Aquascutum and Burberrys, both of which claim to have invented the style. Whatever the truth may be, the trench coats made by these two companies (see p. 80) are of equally fine quality, and both offer the cream-coloured town coat, usually lined with tartan. If you go to Burberrys, however, you can have your initials embroidered inside the coat if you're that keen to impress your friends. To keep your coat waterproof, be sure to have it treated when you have it dry-cleaned.

TIMELESS TWEED

Where would British elegance be without its legendary tweed? The most famous and finest of fabrics made in the United Kingdom is certainly Harris Tweed, which is primarily used for jackets. This cloth comes exclusively from the eponymous island in the Outer Hebrides, which are to the north of Scotland. It's made from pure virgin Irish or Scottish sheepswool, using traditional methods, and comes in three thicknesses: standard (perfect for autumn and winter jackets), light (used for summer clothes) and bantam, for hot climates (if you want to take a trip

A LITTLE TOUR OF MEN'S FASHIONS

If it's a shirt you're looking for, there's no better place to go to than Jermyn Street. It crosses St James Street, where you'll find, almost side-by-side, the ultra-classy shops of Lobb and Lock. North of Piccadilly, you'll find Savile Row, where the bespoke tailors are congregated. A walk down nearby Regent Street will enable you to visit the large stores of Aquascutum and Austin Reed, whose Art Deco hairdresser's and barber's shop is listed as being of special historical interest.

down the Nile or dress up like an officer in the Indian army).

HATS: FROM BOWLERS TO PANAMAS

The bowler hat was invented in 1850 by a farmer called William Coke to prevent his gamekeepers' heads from being struck by stray branches, but it was in London that these famous hats truly came into their own. Although rather outmoded these days, they used to be part of the uniform adopted by workers in the City or the civil service. Of course the bowler really owes its immortality to Charlie Chaplin. If you don't want to look like the little tramp himself, or like John Steed from the TV series *The Avengers*, you could always get yourself a trilby, a cap, a deerstalker or a timeless panama for the summer from Lock (see p. 90).

NEW BRITISH CUISINE

British food has had a pretty poor press over the years. Memories of vegetables boiled into submission and over-cooked meat die hard. But there's been a culinary revolution. In London there are now shoals of smart, stylish restaurants with original cuisine from real Greek to Pacific fusion. You can still find the traditional dishes and beverages of Olde Englande but they have been rejuvenated to suit the palates of Cool Britannia. Today's cooking is more confidently flavoured, with a slick of oil, a squeeze of garlic, a scattering of fresh herbs and fragrant spices, a time bomb of chilli and plenty of ripe, robust English cheeses.

TEA

Time was when tea was a 'cuppa'. It was made from the leaves of the tea plant, a bush that grows on hillsides

in India, Sri Lanka, China and Africa. It was bought loose or in packets, and made in teapots. Then came the teabag revolution and a cargo of blends for all times of the day, like breakfast

or afternoon tea. Speciality teas flavoured with different essences were followed by an orchard of fruit teas. But tea-time is still sacred in the British psyche, along with cucumber sandwiches, tea-cakes, crumpets and fairy cakes, and nothing beats a cream tea with scones and clotted cream.

FOOD ON THE RUN

The explosion of fast food outlets was led by the American chains, the inevitable MacDonalds and their ham-burger-peddling competitors and Colonel Sanders' Kentucky Fried Chicken. But the city has several hundred pizza or pasta chains which will satisfy ravenous children. Sandwiches are the 'new hamburgers', and most supermarkets sell pre-packed sandwiches, but the Prêt-à-Manger outlets with their sleek steel floors and cheery staff offer more interesting fillings.

ENGLISH CHEESE

Cheddar and Stilton are the most popular cheeses and washing down a creamy, tangy Stilton with a glass of port is still part of Christmas. Industrially-produced cheese sold in supermarkets all but destroyed the small cheese-maker. But now over four hundred different kinds of cheese are produced by small farms in the UK. They use

PITFIELD'S
1850
SHOREDITCH
ABV 5%
PORTER

BANGERS AND BEER

The great British sausage, which was much maligned for many years, has once again become stylish, so much so that bangers and mash have found their way onto the menus of many smart restaurants and pubs. Traditional butchers are making their own sausages again and the classic pork or beef sausage is now vying with others made of venison or wild boar. The **Portwine** family butchers has been in Covent Garden for the last 230 years; 24 Earlham St., WC2 ☎ 020 7836 2353.

A. S. Portwine & Son

Brits used to drink bitter, flat and tepid, which was traditionally brewed in wooden casks. It had a job to hold its own against the paler, fizzier, chilled Continental or Australian lagers that offered a cool new means of intoxication. The pub crowd couldn't give a XXXX for the old brews until the Campaign for Real Ale made its mark. Try **the Pitfield Beer Shop**, Pitfield Street, N1 ☎ 020 7739 3701 makes an original bitter or Eco Warrior, an organic beer, or go to **O'Hanlon's** pub, 8 Tysoe St, ☎ 020 7739 3701 to try their award-winning Dry Stout.

cow's, sheep's or goat's milk, sometimes unpasteurized, and produce a kaleidescope of flavours. Remarkable when it all comes from the same basic natural product. A cheese from Neal's Yard Dairy, 17 Shorts Gardens, Covent Garden, makes a perfect present.

MAD COWS AND ORGANIC FOOD ENTHUSIASTS

British beef is very strictly monitored nowadays following a series of scares about mad cows and E-coli. Scottish Aberdeen Angus is one of the best kinds of beef in the world, and there has been a whirlwind of demand for free-range beef fed on grass. With the meat scares, came a sharp rise in vegetarianism, and you'll find a variety of good vegetarian restaurants serving inventive, delicious and often inexpensive food. That rise was surpassed by a boom in organic food. The supermarkets can't get enough of it and some chefs refuse to use anything but organic ingredients in their kitchens.

FISH 'N' CHIPS

Fish and chips is the original British fast food to eat on the move. It's cheap and nutritious. The fish is usually either cod or haddock, and the portions of chips should be huge. Traditionally served in newspaper, drenched in malt vinegar and scattered with salt, they're eaten with the fingers. Absolutely delicious, but don't count the calories.

LONDON, CAPITAL OF CULTURE

No-one could hope to experience a fraction of the cultural life of London in a weekend. The West End shows and straight theatre are world renowned, there's a thriving dance and classical music scene and some of the finest and most unusual museums and galleries you'll ever visit.

CAPITAL OF FREE THINKING

A great many artists, writers and other historical figures have found both inspiration and a safe haven in London. Karl Marx wrote *Das Kapital* here and is buried in Highgate cemetery, and when Sigmund Freud fled from Vienna after the Nazi German invasion in 1938, this is where he came. Visit the Freud Museum, 20 Maresfield Gdns, NW3 ☎ 020 7435 20 02, Wed.-Sun.

noon-5pm. Claude Monet, the French painter, took refuge here, famously painting Westminster Bridge. The great musician Georg Friedrich Händel, took British

Karl Marx at work in London.

citizenship in 1726, while Richard Wagner conducted the orchestra at the Royal Albert Hall in 1877. The American writers Mark Twain and Henry James were also visitors. Mahatma Gandhi studied law here and went on to lead the struggle for Indian independence, while London gave British novelist Salman Rushdie, also of Indian origin, the right conditions for his creativity.

CONTEMPORARY ART

To mark the year 2000 and the opening of Tate Modern, a new gallery (25 Sumner Street, Bankside, SE1 ☎ 020 7887 8000, Sun.-Thu. 10am-6pm, Fri.-Sat. 10am-10pm), the first new pedestrian bridge over the Thames will be inaugurated. It will span the

Millennium Bridge by Norman Foster.

Thames from St Paul's Cathedral to the Tate Modern, which will house the glories of 20th century art and exhibit new art as it's created. The renamed Tate Britain (every day 10am-6pm, Millbank, SW1 ☎ 020 7887 8000), awards the Turner Prize to one of the finest British artists of the moment. Exhibitions by artists such as Gilbert & George can be seen at the Anthony d'Offay

19th-century French caricature of Richard Wagner.

Gallery (9, 21, 23 and 24 Dering St., Mon.-Fri. 10am-5.30pm, Sat. 10am-1pm). The Chisenhale Studios generally show work by British artists (64 Chisenhale Rd, E3 ☎ 020 8981 1916, every day 1-6pm). For the most arresting photographs, make your way to the

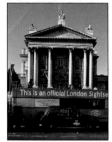

Photographer's Gallery (5 and 8 Great Newport St., WC2 ☎ 020 7831 1772, Mon.-Sat 11am-6pm, Sun. noon-6pm).

THEATRE

With a hundred or so theatres in London, the nation has kept faith with the traditions of William Shakespeare. The Royal Shakespeare Company (Barbican Centre ☎ 020 7638 8891) keeps the bard's works in its repertory, but for a more lifelike Elizabethan performance, go to Shakespeare's Globe (New Globe Walk, Bankside, SE1 ☎ 020 7401 9919, www.shakespeare-globe.org), which is also open for visits. The Royal National Theatre (South Bank,

Modern furniture at the Tate Britain.

SE1 ☎ 020 7452 3000) concentrates on the classical repertoire. The West End theatres around Shaftesbury Avenue provide musicals and shows for a wider audience.

MUSIC

London's orchestras are world renowned. The Royal Albert Hall (☎ 020 7589 8212), where the Promenade concerts are performed July-September, is home to the equally celebrated Royal Philharmonic Orchestra, conducted by Daniele Gatti. The London Symphony Orchestra, under Sir Colin Davies, is at the Barbican Hall, Silk Street, EC2 ☎ 020 7638 8891. The Royal Festival Hall, Southbank, (☎ 020 7960 4242) is the home of the London Philharmonic Orchestra. At the dazzling new Royal

Opera House, Covent Garden (☎ 020 7304 4000) opera is performed in the original language, while the English National Opera, St Martin's Lane, (☎ 020 7632 8300) produces opera of international standard in English.

UNUSUAL MUSEUMS

Visit **Madame Tussaud's** (Marylebone Rd, NW1 ⊖ Baker St. ☎ 020 7935 6861) to see the famous wax works. Imitators include the **Rock Circus** (London Pavilion, 1 Piccadilly Circus, W1 ⊖ Piccadilly Circus ☎ 020 7734 7203), which has models of pop stars. If the kids have always wanted to read the news, try **BBC Experience**, (Broadcasting House W1, ⊖ Oxford Circus ☎ 0870 603 0304), Mon. 10am-4.30 or 11-4.30pm.

MULTI-CULTURAL LONDON

COLOURS OF THE INDIAN SUBCONTINENT

London is home to Europe's largest communities from the Indian subcontinent, with 525,000 Indians and Pakistanis. The Bengalis now inhabit Brick Lane, just east of the City, formerly the Jewish quarter and refuge to immigrant communities since the early 18th century. Southall, with its large Sikh community, will plunge you into the exotic east with its colourful fabrics and jewellery. The district's restaurants are little gems in themselves and absolutely not to be missed.

CHINATOWN

For more than thirty years, the Soho district around Gerrard Street (see p. 41) has been the heart of the Chinese community. Many of its 55,000 members came originally from Hong Kong. If you can get to London in late January, you may have a chance to join in the festivities of the Chinese New Year, during which groups of men dressed as dragons

B eneath its lowering grey skies, London offers you a riot of colours and smells, reflecting the city's colonial heritage and the links it still maintains with the distant lands which, since their independence, have come together under the auspices of the Commonwealth. This coexistence of communities of widely different origins is the source of London's cosmopolitan character, fostered by a long tradition of free-thinking and openness. For all these reasons and more, a trip to London is also a trip around the world, from the familiar to the strange and back again.

BLACK RHYTHMS

Jamaicans make up the majority of London's 450,000-strong Afro-Caribbean community. To get a feel of its atmosphere, try visiting Brixton's lively market (see p. 102). If it's something more hip and trendy you're after, some of the coolest 'black clubs' are to be found in Dalston, around Ridley Road (E8). And London's Afro-Caribbean festival, the Notting Hill Carnival, is the biggest carnival in Europe. More than 500,000 people flood into the area over the last weekend in August to watch a truly wild parade, or to join in and dance the time away to the competing sounds of soul and reggae.

the Virgin Mary. This takes place at the church of St Peter in Clerkenwell, and is attended by a great many of the 75,000 Italians living in London. The Jewish community is settled around Golders Green, St John's Wood and Hampstead. When the Second World War broke out, many Poles also sought refuge in the city, and their numbers have now swollen to around 50,000.

The French Lycée in London.

There are enough Germans in London for there to be a German school, and many French people congregate around South Kensington and send their children to the French Lycée.

roam the area to drive away evil spirits.

IMAMS AND MOSQUES

Muslims make up both the largest (there are currently 800,000 living in the UK) and most diverse community in London, ranging from oil-rich sheiks from the Gulf States to longer-term immigrants from East Africa and Pakistan. There are mosques in different parts of the city, including Regent's Park, with its copper cupola, and the East London Mosque in Whitechapel Road. The latter was largely funded by Arab donors and reflects a harmonious mix of modern design and traditional architecture.

ST PATRICK'S DAY

Westminster Cathedral (Morpeth Terrace, SW1) and St Patrick's Church (Soho Square, W1) are two of the main rallying points for London's 250,000-strong Irish community. Every year on St Patrick's Day, they crowd into the city's churches and pubs to toast their patron saint, who freed Ireland from snakes.

THE EUROPEAN COMMUNITY

On 16 July, the Italian community come together for a big procession in honour of

---

MULTI-CULTURAL EXHIBITS

The Victoria and Albert Museum, (Cromwell Road, SW7, ☎ 020 7938 8500, every day 10am-5.45pm) has a significant collection of artefacts from the Indian sub-continent as part of its permanent collection.
The Jewish Museum, (Raymond Burton House, 129-131 Albert Street, NW1 ☎ 020 7284 1997, www.jewmusm.ort.org, Sun.-Thu 10am-4pm, entry £3), traces the history of the Jewish community in Britain and has a fine collection of Jewish ceremonial art.

ENGLISH CHINA AND PORCELAIN

The manufacture of china in the United Kingdom dates back to the 18th century. Fine English bone china has gained an international reputation. You'll often find complete dinner services at quite reasonable prices. If it's something typically English you're after, how about a plate to hold a large cake, with matching side plates from which to eat the slices? Or, better still, a cake-stand consisting of two or more plates, one above the other and used for serving smaller cakes at tea-time?

CHINA

Western European china is a refinement of medieval glazed pottery. The raw clay is shaped in a mould or on the wheel and allowed to dry. It's then placed in the kiln to fire. When it's cool, it's glazed and fired again in the kiln at a high temperature for at least 30 hours in order to set the design. These days you'll find the finest pieces of old china in antique shops, but modern china, often decorated with floral patterns or English landscapes in reds or pale blues, is of high quality and provides good value for money. Crockery of this type doesn't require any special treatment and can be put in the

dishwasher with no problems. China that shouldn't go in a dishwasher is clearly marked.

BONE CHINA

Porcelain, or bone china, owes its whiteness and translucence to the fine white clay known as kaolin from which it's made. Porcelain was first produced in China and was taken up by European manufacturers in the 18th century. Innovations were then introduced in England, including the addition of bone ash to the clay. This process, invented in 1800, gave the fine porcelain known as bone china its name. Bone china pieces are fired twice. The first firing often lasts 24 hours and fixes the gleaming, glassy coating of glaze. In the second firing, at high or low temperatures, colours and designs are permanently fixed.

SPODE

Spode, the famous English porcelain factory, was first established in 1770. It was founded by Josiah Spode, who later developed the art of making bone china in 1800. The elegant china it produces is still very highly prized and there are two very delicate classic designs: *Stafford Flowers*, which was created in the early 19th century and features designs inspired by botanical drawings, and *Blue Italian* porcelain, which is decorated with pastoral scenes in blue and white. Early pieces can be very valuable.

ROYAL WORCESTER

In the 18th century, this factory was one of England's main manufacturers of porcelain. It was at this time that it began to increase the volume and improve the robustness of its crockery production.

This approach is still maintained today and is reflected in the design of Royal Worcester oven-to-tableware, which stands up equally well to use in the microwave, traditional oven and freezer. Royal Doulton also produces high-quality, durable crockery.

WEDGWOOD, FIRST NAME IN FINE BONE CHINA.

The Wedgwood factory went into production in 1750, and its earliest creations were imitations of precious stones. Between 1764 and 1774, Josiah Wedgwood, the factory's founder, developed creamware,

a fine white porcelain to rival that produced in the factories of Sèvres and Meissen. Later, Wedgwood developed an unglazed black biscuit or basalt pottery, which gave rise to wonderful black and white designs, followed in the 19th century by the famous blue and white. These original creations are still in production today, along with hundreds of other tableware designs, all of a similarly refined quality.

On the base of any piece of china, you'll find the factory's trademark, given either in letters or as a monogram. The more prestigious the brand, the more expensive the piece will be. Rarer or more exceptional pieces are also marked with the artist's signature or the stamp of the workshop in which they were decorated. These things are important, as they'll be noted by prospective buyers should you later choose to sell them.

BIG CHECKS AND LITTLE FLOWERS

London is the perfect destination for anyone who loves to sew. In this city, you'll find fabrics to suit every need, from upholstery to dressmaking, at reasonable prices and often with unbeatable designs. Woollens are not particularly cheap, but their range and quality are such that you could select them with your eyes closed and still not be disappointed.

for official ceremonies, weddings, or by Scottish fans at rugby matches. There are several hundred different patterns. The tartans of the Campbell, Leslie and MacArthur clans are predominantly green, while those of the Hays, Frazers, MacFies and Wallaces are dominated by red. Tartan makes a perfect furnishing fabric, creating an atmosphere that is at once rustic and luxurious. You could use light tartan silk to

TARTANS: FROM HIGHLAND CLANS TO RUGBY FANS

Tartan is a reversible, checked cloth of woollen twill worn mainly in Scotland, but also in Ireland. Before the 12th century, tartan had a social significance, enabling the members of different clans to be identified by the pattern of tartan they wore. The cloth is used in the making of kilts, which are today worn mainly

float at your windows, cover your old armchair in a thick, warm tartan twill, or choose a tartan carpet to add a touch of Scottish style to your corridor or the stairs

A CHINTZ FOR ALL SEASONS

Chintz is a generic term used to refer to fabrics printed with a floral design. Originally imported from India in the 16th and 17th century, they were copied and manufactured in Britain after 1680. At first, chintz motifs were used mainly for furnishings, but were later adapted for use in wallpaper designs by companies such as Laura Ashley and Colefax and Fowler.

You'll also find excellent chintz fabrics with the Liberty label for making clothes of different kinds.

SOFT AND GENTLE AS A LAMB

Shetland and lambswool are the yarns of choice for knitting a perfect everyday pullover, the kind you like to wear again and again and which becomes more comfortable the longer you wear it. Shetland wool is

a very strong, warm yarn, covered in soft down, taken from the sheep farmed in the Shetland Islands to the north of Scotland. Shetland jumpers traditionally come in timeless designs: turtle- or v-necks in classic shades, though these days you'll find them in fashion colours, too. Go for a very close knit, which will last you much longer.

Lambswool is softer and finer than Shetland wool. Lambswool double-knit yarn is very strong and can be machine-washed. Lambswool jumpers from Marks and Spencer, for example, are of excellent quality, particularly the men's range, which includes some designs in truly wonderful chiné colours.

FOR THOSE IN PERIL ON THE SEA

To be truly authentic, Arran jumpers should be knitted by hand from pale-coloured or unbleached wool in a pattern that includes a thick rib or cable design. On this Scottish island, which lies in the Clyde estuary to the west of Glasgow, these warm, hard-wearing sweaters were traditionally made by the Arran fisherman's wife in order to enable her to identify

her husband's body if he were drowned at sea. Each woman would knit her own uniquely recognisable pattern, which is why these jumpers are known as 'fisherman's sweaters'.

COLEFAX AND FOWLER

39 Brook St., W1
☎ 020 7493 22 31
⊖ Bond Street
Mon.-Fri. 9.30am-5.30pm.

The collection of chintz fabrics sold by this establishment is one of the finest in the whole of London. In particular, you'll find reproductions of 19th-century motifs, and new designs are brought out every year to add to the already impressive catalogue. The interior design of this shop is like an English country house, with every window swagged and every table and cushion sporting ruffles and chintz.

OUTDOOR LONDON

Trailing round noisy streets, battling with the crowds or craning your neck to look at another impressive monument can be fun – for a while. The city's parks are there to soothe your jangled nerves and pacify the children. London is one of the greenest capitals in the world. The Royal Parks were formerly the hunting grounds of royalty, and between them St James' Park, Green Park, Hyde Park and Kensington Gardens cover 312 hectares/771 acres, right in the centre of the city.

FROM ST JAMES'S PARK TO KENSINGTON GARDENS

St James's Park was opened to the public by Charles II. The park we see today was designed for King George IV by John Nash, creating the lake, winding paths and floral shrubberies. Duck island is home to many wild breeds of beautiful ducks and children crowd round at feeding time, 4pm daily, to watch the exotic birds squabble over their feed. There's a children's playground and, in summer, bands give concerts in the bandstands. Green Park was once a swampy burial ground for lepers. It became fashionable in 1730, when Queen Caroline ordered the planting of trees for the Queen's Walk. It's particularly famous for its tree-lined avenues. Hyde Park is the biggest park. William III ordered Rotten Row, originally the 'Route du Roi', to be lit with 300 oil lamps to protect horsemen and carriages from thieves. You can still ride along Rotten Row and there are two stables with qualified instructors. (☎ 020 7723 2813). The Serpentine lake winds its way across Hyde Park. In summer you can hire boats and pedalos (☎ 020 262 1330) or cool off at the Lido swimming area (☎ 020 7298 2100). You can play tennis and football or jog, and some areas have been specially designated for roller-blading and skating. The musical highlight of the summer is the open-air relay of the Last Night of the Promenade concerts ('Proms'), from the Royal Albert Hall. Kensington Gardens was a poignant focal point after the death of Diana, Princess of Wales and there are plans for a Diana Garden and Diana Walk, starting from her home in Kensington Palace.

GARDENS AND SHOWS

The Chelsea Physik Garden 66 Royal Hospital Road, SW3 (☎ 020 352 5646) was established in 17th century to grow medicinal herbs. It's open to the public in the summer. In May, The Royal

St James's Park, view from the bridge across to Whitehall.

Horticultural Society holds the Chelsea Flower show (0870 534 4444) in the grounds of the Royal Hospital, next door.

WATERWAYS

One of the most pleasant ways to see London is from a river boat, passing all the major sights on the way to the Tower or the Thames Barrier via Canary Wharf and the Millennium Dome. Catamaran Cruises (☎ 020 7987 1185) leave from Embankment Pier, and City Cruises (☎ 020 7237 5134) leave from Westminster Pier, as do Campion Launches (☎ 020 8305 0300) and Thames Cruises (☎ 020 930 3373).

THE LONDON EYE

Towering an impressive 135m/443ft above the Thames, the impressive London Eye, Jubilee Gardens, South Bank, SE1, (☎ 0870 5000 600) has made a big impact on the capital's skyline. It gives a bird's-eye view of London from Windsor to Dartford in a 30-minute 'flight'. Departures daily 10am-6pm in winter or 9am-dusk in summer, adults £7.45, children £4.95.

FOOTBALL CRAZY

Many children live, breathe and dream football. The FA Premier League Hall of Fame, (Riverside Building,

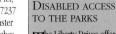

T he Liberty Drives offer the elderly, disabled and infirm free rides in Hyde Park in electrically powered buggies driven by trained volunteers. Two of the buggies are specially designed to carry wheelchair-bound passengers. There are clearly marked collection and delivery points on the park's perimeter.
☎ 0498 498096.

Westminster Bridge Road, ☎ 0870 848 8484, adults £9.95, children £6.40) is a celebration of 'the beautiful game' past, present and future. The collection of memorabilia

goes back over 100 years and includes a Victorian leather football. There are waxworks of today's stars and an interactive virtual stadium.

LONDON ZOO

London Zoo, (Regent's Park, NW1 ☎ 020 722 3333. Every day 10am-4pm in winter, 10am-5.30pm in summer, adults £9, children £7) is one of the most famous in the world. It's home to over 600 species of rare and beautiful animals, from elephants to tigers, and from penguins to piranhas. The Web of Life, housed in a glass pavilion, is a new interactive exhibit that brings people close to animals from ants to anteaters.

The London Eye.

What to see Practicalities

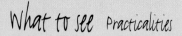

Light Railway). which will help you to keep costs down. You can purchase them from underground stations or newsagents. A daily Travelcard for two zones costs £3.90 and is valid after 9.30am during the week, and all day on Saturday and Sunday. The Weekend Travelcard gives you discounted travel for two days, and the Family card is the cheapest way to travel around for a pair of adults with up to 4 children. You can buy Visitor Travelcards from travel agents prior to your departure for London.

THE TUBE

The London Underground, the Tube, is the easiest – and cheapest – way to get around. There's a map on the inside back cover of this guide which will show you how easy it is to get about. You buy tickets at the Tube stations where there are automatic machines or, if you don't have the right change, go to the ticket counter. If you want to check your route, there are always large-scale maps in the stations.

GETTING AROUND IN LONDON

London is a vast city and you can't hope to see all of it in one day. The most important sights are often far apart.

You can get around the city using the underground – or 'Tube' – trains, buses and taxis, as well as the overground rail network for destinations outside the centre, in Greater London.

TRAVELCARDS

There are all sorts of budget travel cards for bus, underground and train (including the Docklands

The tube system is divided into 6 zones, but most of the sites or shops you're likely to visit will be in zones 1 and 2. A single adult ticket for zones 1 and 2 costs £1.80, and 80p for a child. A cheaper way of getting around is to buy a zone 1 and 2 One-Day Travelcard for £3.90. It's valid from 9.30am and you can use it as many times as you like on tubes and buses. The Family Travelcard, also valid from 9.30am, is cheaper still. An adult's ticket costs £2.60 and a child's ticket costs 80p. The group must be of 1-2 adults, and there can be 1-4 children. The only limitation is that the group can't split up and travel separately.

The Tube also provides the fastest way to get around the city. Trains run from 5.30am to midnight, except on Christmas Day. Lines and directions are clearly signposted. Although you can get a free pocket-map at the ticket office and there are large-scale maps on the platforms, if you have any doubts don't hesitate to ask a member of staff as they're always helpful. Waiting times and destinations for the next few trains are shown on indicator boards on each platform. Be sure to keep your ticket, as you'll need to use it to leave the system on reaching your destination.

BUSES

The buses are slower than the tube, but they allow you to see the city, particularly if you sit upstairs in a double-decker, the famous two-storey London bus. On most buses, you show your Travelcard or

buy a ticket from the driver as you get on, though on some older-style buses you sit down and pay a conductor who'll come and ask you where you're going and sell you a ticket. Buses are a good way to get around at night. Night

buses display a large 'N' before the number, and the service runs between 11 pm and 6 am. Some buses that you may find particularly useful include the 15, which will take you from the British Museum to South Kensington

TAXIS

There are two types of taxi plying their trade in London, black cabs and minicabs. Black cabs are easy to recognise by their shape, though some of them have swapped their traditional black for another shade or a multicoloured advertisement.

When the taxi is free the yellow light on the roof is lit up and there's a sign inside saying 'For Hire'. You should allow £1.40 as a basic minimum, plus 20 pence per minute or 242m/265yd (every 161m/176yd once the fare has risen to £9). Luggage, additional passengers and night travel are all charged extra.

Minicabs are privately-owned cars which offer their services directly, particularly at night, when there aren't so many black cabs on the streets. If you decide to take a minicab, make sure you ask the price of your journey before you get in the car, or call a cab belonging to a taxi company, such as Lady's Cabs (for women on their own) ☎ 020 7254 3501.

If you leave something in a taxi by mistake, you can call the lost property office ☎ 020 7833 0996, but the office is only open Mon.–Fri., 9am–4pm.

via Piccadilly Circus, the 168, which goes from Oxford Street or Piccadilly Circus to St Paul's, and the 77A, which goes from Charing Cross to Westminster. To stop a bus, hold out your arm so the driver can see.

SIGHTSEEING BY BUS OR BOAT

Taking a tour on an open-top bus is a good way to orientate yourself and locate the major sites. There's a live English commentary by trained guides or digitally recorded commentary. The Big Bus Company ☎ 020 7233 9533, or Original London Sightseeing Tour, both offer hop-on, hop-off tours with tickets valid for 24 hours. Or you can see London from the river. Starting from Westminster Pier, at the foot of Big Ben, boats go east to the Tower of London, Greenwich or Millennium Dome, and some go west to Kew, Richmond and Hampton Court. Some charter operators offer Evening Dinner Cruises. London Travel information has more details ☎ 020 7222 1234.

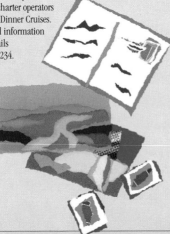

USING THE TELEPHONE

All London telephone numbers now have eight digits, beginning with either 7 (for inner London) or 8 (for outer London). To call a number from within the city, you must dial all eight digits, but if you call from outside London you must dial 020 before your number. Calls are cheaper after 6pm on weekdays and throughout the weekend.

Public telephones take coins, (10p, 20p, 50p and £1), phone cards or credit cards, and you can often use any one of the above in the same telephone. The old traditional red booths have mostly been replaced by modern, see-through boxes. Telephones usually have instructions for use, but the instructions aren't uniform. Some phones require you to put money in first, some after dialling, or sometimes coins must be inserted when the call is answered. Phone cards are available from newsagents and post offices. Cards come with different values, starting at £2. If you have problems, call the operator on 100, or 155 for international calls. If you need to find a number, call directory enquiries on 192, or for international numbers call 153.

You can dial international calls from any phone box. First dial 00, then the country code, then the area code followed by the number. To call the United States or Canada, dial 00-1, Australia 00-61 and New Zealand 00-64.

WRITING HOME

When you're writing home, it's easy to buy stamps. They're on sale at newsagents or from post offices (open Mon.-Fri., 9am-5.30pm, Sat. 9am-12.30pm). The central Trafalgar Square Post Office (24-28 William IV Street, WC2 ☎ 020 7930 9580 is open Mon-Fri 8am-8pm and Sat. 9am-8pm.

The large red postboxes are easy to spot. It will cost 38p for a postcard or 44p for a letter to Australia, New Zealand, Canada or the US.

INTERNET CAFÉS

Keeping in touch through the internet is increasingly simple, and there's a proliferation of cafés with an atmosphere that's all their own. Try Buzz Bar, 95 Portobello Road, W11 ☎ 020 7460 4906 ⊖ Ladbroke Grove or Notting Hill Gate, open Mon.-Fri. 10am-9pm, Sat. 10am-6pm, Sun. noon-7pm. Net access: 10p per minute. e-mail: buzzbar@hotmail.com. Web: www.portobellogold. com. Or, situated in a more central location, try Global Café, Waterstone's 4th floor,

203-206 Piccadilly, SW1 ☎ 020 7287 2242. ⊖ Piccadilly Circus, Open Mon.-Fri. 8am-11pm, Sat. 10am-11pm, Sun. noon-11pm. Net access: £5 for 60 minutes (charged per 5-minute unit). e-Mail: dbcox@hotmail.com. Web: www.gold.globalcafe.co.uk.

BANKS AND BUREAUX DE CHANGE

Banks are open Monday–Friday, 9.30am-4pm, and some are also open on Saturdays until noon. Most branches in central London have cash machines from which you can get money 24-hours a day.

If you don't have a card and need to change money out of banking hours, there are many Bureaux de Change (Thomas Cook or Cheque Point) in the tourist areas, but you'll usually get a poorer rate than from the cash machine or bank, and they'll also charge commission.

**Cheque Point
548 Oxford St., W1
☎ 020 7723 1005
⊖ Marble Arch
open 24 hours.**

**HSBC Belgravia
Belgravia Branch,
89 Buckingham Palace Rd,
SW1
☎ 020 7699 1400**

**TTT Foreign Exchange
Corporation
35 Long Acre, WC2
☎ 020 7836 9000**

**TTT Foreign Exchange
Corporation
4 Sloane St., SW1
☎ 020 7699 1400 or
020 7235 7021**

**The Money Corporation
18 Piccadilly, W1
☎ 020 7439 2100**

OPENING TIMES FOR MUSEUMS AND MONUMENTS

Museums and monuments are usually open 10am–5pm. Some, such as the British Museum, don't open until 2pm or 2.30pm on Sundays. Opening times don't change much between summer and winter. They're open every weekday, but all are closed on 24-26 December and Good Friday, but it's always best to check.

The attraction pass Go See offers unlimited access to 17 major museums and galleries, including the Hayward Gallery, Imperial War Museum, Royal Academyof Arts, Tower Bridge Experience, Science Museum and Victoria and Albert Museum. You can buy the cards at participating attractions or the Tourist Information Centre. An adult 3-day pass is £16, and a family pass (2 adults and up to 4 children) is £32. It's worth checking whether it's worth your while for what you want to see, because some museums and monuments are free.

Westminster and royal London

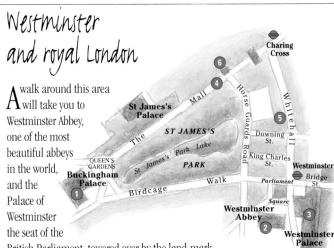

A walk around this area will take you to Westminster Abbey, one of the most beautiful abbeys in the world, and the Palace of Westminster the seat of the British Parliament, towered over by the land-mark clocktower with the world-famous chimes of Big Ben. A walk through St James's Park takes you to the royal palaces of St James's Palace and Buckingham Palace. You'll find it impossible to avoid the crowds drawn by the Changing of the Guard ceremony that takes place outside the residence of the Queen in the mornings.

❶ Buckingham Palace ★★★

The Mall
Credit card bookings
☎ **020 7321 2233**
Timed admissions every day,
Aug.-Sep. 9.30am-4.15pm,
£10.50. Changing of the
Guard every day 11.30am,
every other day in winter.
☎ **0891 505452.**

The famous residence of the British Queen dates from the early 19th century (except for the façade, which was built in 1913). The architect John Nash transformed the original manor house (1702) into a vast palace, originally intended as a simple *pied-à-terre* for King George IV. To fund restoration work after a fire damaged Windsor castle, some state rooms are open to the public in the summer while the Queen is on holiday.

❷ Westminster Abbey ★★★

Broad Sanctuary, SW1
☎ **020 7222 5897**
Mon.-Fri. 9.30am-3.45pm,
Sat. 9.30am-1.45pm,
No visits on Sunday, though
the Chapter House is open.

Begin by admiring the abbey's fine exterior with its flying

buttresses. Once inside, visitors in a hurry should go first to the sanctuary – to see the splendid stained glass – and the chapel of Henry VII, with its extraordinary vaulted ceiling. If you go to the Abbey Museum, with its effigies of the dead, take a good look at Henry VII's face and you'll see a few hairs above his ears.

Apparently they were caught in the cast when his death mask was being made. This was originally a substantial church foundation. The Chapter House and cloister court are also worth visiting.

❸ Palace of Westminster★★★

Parliament Square, SW1
☎ **020 7219 3000.**
House of Commons
Mon.-Thu. 2.30-10pm,
Wed. 9.30am-10pm,
Fri. 9.30am-3pm.
Book a long time in advance for the House of Lords.

The palace of Westminster is a neo-Gothic building dating from the 19th century. It houses both the House of Commons and the House of Lords. It's the heart of British political life. Inside 300 or so people work in around 1,000 offices, and there are nearly 2 miles/3 km of corridors. The palace is best known for its clocktower bell, affectionately known as Big Ben (the nickname of Benjamin Hall, who was in charge of its installation in the tower). You can go up into the tower to see the bell's

mechanism, as long as you don't mind the long climb up the stairs. The famous chimes of Big Ben can be heard within a radius of 3 km/2 miles of Westminster.

❹ The Mall★★

The Mall was fashionable back in 1660, though at that time it was an ordinary tree-lined avenue. It wasn't until 1911 that the wide avenue we see today was created by the architect who also designed the Admiralty Arch in Queen Victoria's honour. The Mall runs along one side of St James's Park (open daily 6am-midnight), London's oldest park and one of its most pleasant. In the 19th century, cows grazed here. Today ornamental ducks, black swans and pelicans swim on the lake.

❺ Whitehall★★★

Walking down Whitehall towards Trafalgar Square, you pass Downing Street on your left. You can no longer walk down it for security reasons, but on the left you'll see one façade of the Foreign Office and on your right, number 10, the official residence of the Prime Minister. Along Whitehall are the Departments of State, including the Treasury, the Cabinet Office, and the old Admiralty.

❻ THE INSTITUTE OF CONTEMPORARY ARTS

Carlton House Terrace, The Mall
☎ **020 7873 0051 Open every day noon-9.30pm**
e-mail: tickets@ica.ork.uk.

Sponsored by Toshiba, the ICA stages exhibitions of avant-garde art from both Britain and around the world. Make sure you visit the bookshop to buy a copy of *Frieze*, one of the most impressive art magazines you could hope to read, before relaxing for a while in the bar. Very pleasant.

From Piccadilly Circus to Green Park

Piccadilly is one of the smartest areas to shop in London. It symbolises the more expensive and elegant aspects of the city. As you walk along it, you'll find Wedgwood, Simpsons and Fortnum and Mason. Piccadilly is far less crowded, more stylish and more expensive than Oxford Street, so you can be be more relaxed about your shopping. Jermyn Street is a must for gentleman's outfitters, especially hand-made shirts and shoes, and St James Street is home to many of the Queen's suppliers. Savile Row, famous for bespoke tailored suits, is just off Regent Street.

❶ Piccadilly Circus★★

This is almost certainly one of the most famous places in London. The statue of Eros with his bow and arrow seems to be aiming provocatively at passers-by and the various strange-looking types who gather round his fountain. Piccadilly Circus is best visited at night, when all the signs are

on and flashing away. Be sure not to miss Tower Records, the gigantic record shop that stays open till midnight, where you're sure to find the track you heard in the club the night before.

❷ St James's Church★★

197 Piccadilly
☎ **020 7734 4511**
Open every day 9am-6pm.

Built by Christopher Wren in 1684, this lovely church hosts the weddings of the London

gentry. In the later part of the week (Thu., Fri. and Sat. 10am-6pm) there's a flea market in the grounds. Concerts are often given in the church which has a splendid accoustic for choral and vocal music. You can have a coffee at Aroma which replaced the old Wren Coffee House.

❸ MacKenzie's★★

169 Piccadilly, W1
☎ **020 7495 5514**
Mon.-Tue., Thu.-Fri. 10am-6.30pm, Wed. 10am-7pm, Sat. 10am-6pm. Sun. noon-5pm.

Scarves, jumpers, kilts, tartan cloth by the metre, in other words all the fundamental classics of British clothing you could ever dream of taking home with you. What makes this shop so unusual is the truly exceptional

warmth and politeness you find on stepping inside.

❹ The Royal Academy of Arts★★
Burlington House, Piccadilly, W1
☎ 020 7439 7438
www.royalacademy.org.uk
Every day 10am-5.30pm, Fri. 10am-8.30pm.

This gallery stages the city's largest temporary exhibitions. The 'Sensation' show, with Damien Hirst's pickled animals and a picture of the Virgin painted with elephant dung, caused a huge scandal. The RA shows are all worth seeing, and the Summer Exhibition is an essential fixture in the calendar. At the very least, make sure you see Michelangelo's *Virgin and Child*.

❺ Fortnum & Mason's★★★
181 Piccadilly, W1
☎ 020 7734 8040
Mon.-Sat. 9.30am-6pm, tea served 3-6pm.

Liveried staff receive all visitors, whether they're buying or not. Fortnum and Mason is famous above all for its tea, which is exported in great quantities, but is worth a visit just for the magnificent displays in the food hall. Here you'll find every British speciality. In the 4th-floor teashop, you'll be served by friendly, patient and very stylish staff.

❻ Burlington Arcade★★★
This is the realm of cashmere, with no less than five specialist shops. The best is N Peal. The men's shop is at no. 71 (☎ 020 7493 0912) and the ladies' shop at 37 (☎ 020 7493 9220, Mon.-Sat. 9.30am-6pm), which has the widest range of different colours and designs. Or you could try Berk, which has three shops at nos. 6, 20

and 46 (☎ 020 7493 0028, Mon.-Sat. 9am-5.30pm), where you'll also find Burberrys. Don't miss The Irish Linen Company, at nos. 35-36 (☎ 020 7493 899, Mon.-Fri. 9.30am-5.45pm, Sat. 10am-5pm, see p. 96) if you want to sleep between the finest sheets in the world.

THE EXCLUSIVE CLUBS OF ST JAMES'S STREET

St James's Street is home to some of the most exclusive clubs in London, whose members belong to the aristocracy. This tradition is still very much alive in England and the district around the Mall and St James's Park has a great number of clubs. Men (very few clubs admit women) go their club to eat, drink and talk with their equals. One of the most famous and select is *Brook's* (on the corner of St James's Street and Park Place). The Carlton Club, at number 69 St James's, is Conservative Party territory. Election to clubs is a lengthy procedure and visitors aren't admitted.

❼ Waterstone's★★
203-206 Piccadilly, W1
☎ 020 7851 2400
Mon.-Sat. 8.30am-11pm.
Sun. noon-6pm.

Housed in the old Simpson's building, London's biggest bookshop opened in September 1999. After you have browsed your way through the seven floors and 80 departments, you can go for a meal in the café/restaurant, sip a cocktail in the juice bar, or even surf the net.

❽ Waterford Wedgwood★★★
173-174 Piccadilly, W1
☎ 020 7629 2614
Mon.-Fri. 9am-6pm.
Sat. 9.30am-6pm.

The famous blue Wedgwood china is a distinctive part of the British heritage. Josiah Wedgwood, an innovative and extremely skilful potter, started the business in the 18th century. The current fine porcelain collection offers a wide range of designs including flowers, animals and, in particular, motifs of neo-Classical and eastern inspiration. In this shop,

you'll also find the famous Waterford crystal ware and the equally celebrated Coalport decorative plates.

❾ The Ritz★★★
Piccadilly, W1
☎ 020 7493 8181
Tea served at 3.30pm and 5pm.

Who hasn't dreamed of taking tea at the Ritz? To turn your dream into reality and sample dainty sandwiches and cakes,

you should book your table at least a week in advance. Don't forget to pack a tie, though the cloakroom attendant will lend you one if necessary.

❿ Turnbull and Asser★★
71-72 Jermyn St. and 23 Berry St., SW1
☎ 020 7808 3000
Mon.-Fri. 9am-6pm,
Sat. 9.30am-6pm.

This establishment includes the Prince of Wales among its customers, which is surely a guarantee of respectability and quality, if not the height of fashion. Here you'll find superb ready-to-wear shirts, priced at around £75 and up. At 23 Berry St., you can order made-to-measure shirts, but you have to order six at a time.

⓫ James Lock & Co.★★★

6 St James's St., SW1
☎ 020 7930 8874.
Mon.-Fri. 9am-5.30pm,
Sat. 9.30am-5.30pm.

Walking into this shop, one of the most famous in St James's Street, you're treading in the footsteps of Beau Brummel and Lord Byron. Both men shopped here, just as the Prince of Wales does today. At Lock's you'll be placing your head in kindly, expert hands.

⓬ John Lobb★★★

9 St James's St., SW1
☎ 020 7930 3664.
Mon.-Fri. 9am-5.30pm, Sat. 9am-4.30pm.

Even if you've neither the time nor money to buy made-to-measure shoes with a lifetime guarantee from Lobb's, make sure you step inside this shop, which is regarded as having one of the finest interiors in the world. In its neighbouring workshop, you can admire the skill of artists at work. And don't forget to cast your eye over the mezzanine floor as well, to see all the styles displayed on lovely wooden stands.

⓭ Royal Doulton★★

167 Piccadilly, W1
☎ 020 7493 9121
Mon.-Sat. 9.30am-6pm.

For nearly two centuries, the reputation of Royal Doulton has rested primarily on their fine porcelain figurines, whose quality is comparable to those produced by Meissen. The best-known designs, which would make excellent gifts, are the 'Fair Ladies'. You'll also find fine china and tableware in this shop.

⓮ Taylor of Old Bond Street★★★

74 Jermyn St., W1
☎ 020 7930 5321
Mon.-Sat. 8.30am-6pm.

Having an old-fashioned shave can be a great self-indulgence. Here they give you the full experience or you can buy all the tools of the trade and shave yourself at home. The shop also specialises in herbal remedies and aromatherapy.

Leicester Square
Going out on the town

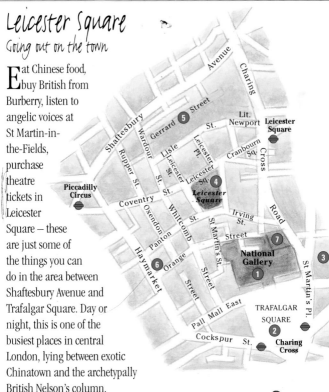

Eat Chinese food, buy British from Burberry, listen to angelic voices at St Martin-in-the-Fields, purchase theatre tickets in Leicester Square – these are just some of the things you can do in the area between Shaftesbury Avenue and Trafalgar Square. Day or night, this is one of the busiest places in central London, lying between exotic Chinatown and the archetypally British Nelson's column.

❶ National Gallery★★★
Trafalgar Square, WC2
☎ 020 7839 3321
www.nationalgallery.org.uk
Mon.-Sat. 10am-6pm,
Wed. 10am–9pm Sun.
noon-6pm. Entry free.

The National Gallery isn't vast, but it contains only masterpieces of European painting from the 13th to the early 20th century, hung in chronological order. 'The Baptism of Christ' by Piero Della Francesca, Holbein's 'The Ambassadors', entire galleries by Rembrandt, 'The Toilet of Venus' by Velazquez and Cézanne's 'Bathers' are all exhibited here.

❷ Trafalgar Square★★★
This monumental square was designed by John Nash in the 1830s. It's dominated by the well-known landmark of Nelson's column (50 m/ 165 ft tall), on which stands

the statue of the famous Admiral Lord Nelson, who was killed during the battle of Trafalgar in 1805. Famed for its pigeons, Trafalgar

Square is a rallying point for political demonstrations, election campaigners and New Year's Eve revellers.

3 St-Martin's-in-the-Field★★
Trafalgar Square, WC2
☎ 020 7930 1862
Mon.-Sat. 8am–6.30pm
Sun. 8am–7.30pm.

This church was built by James Gibbs in 1724. Unlike other churches designed by the same architect, it shows the influence of neo-Classical design rather than the Baroque. Its architecture has been widely imitated. There's a small arts and crafts market (Mon.-Sat. 11am-5pm,

7 THE NATIONAL PORTRAIT GALLERY
St Martin's Place, WC2
☎ 020 7306 0055
Mon.-Sat. 10am-6pm, Sun 12-6pm. Entry free.

The National Portrait Gallery, open at the same times as the National Gallery, offers you a crash course in British history through the faces of its major figures. From kings to artists and heroes to rogues, everyone who's been anyone since the 14th century is hanging on the gallery's walls, including Margaret Thatcher and Mick Jagger.

Sun. noon-5pm). The church is renowned for its world-famous choir, which you can hear on Sundays at 5pm singing choral evensong.

4 Leicester Square★★
The brick façade of the Odeon, an enormous Art Deco cinema, towers above one of the best known squares in London, which is almost entirely devoted to entertainment and shows – mostly films these days – as suggested by the statues of Shakespeare and Charlie Chaplin that have been erected in the middle. There's a very handy kiosk selling discounted theatre tickets for shows the same

day that's well worth a visit. It's open 2.30-6.30pm and all seats are half price, but you have to pay cash.

GERRARD STREET W1
爵禄街
CITY OF WESTMINSTER 西敏寺

5 Gerrard Street★★
Here you're in the heart of London's Chinatown. At the Loong Fu Supermarket, (nos. 42-44), you can buy exotic fruits and other items of food, or drop into one of the many shops selling manga comics or china for an unusual gift to take home. This is also the perfect place to have a Chinese meal for next to nothing. You're spoilt for choice.

6 Burberry of London★★★
18-22 Haymarket, SW1
☎ 020 7930 3343
Mon.-Wed. and Fri. 10am-6pm, Thu. 10am-7pm, Sat. 10am-6pm, Sun. noon-6pm.

Burberry's clothing is more or less guaranteed for life and will outlive any passing

fad. If you don't fancy a mac (£400), try the childrenswear or go for a sweater – it's all top quality.

A walk around Covent Garden

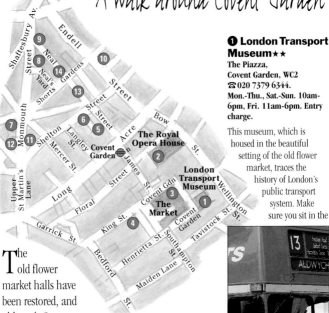

❶ London Transport Museum★★

The Piazza,
Covent Garden, WC2
☎ 020 7379 6344.
Mon.-Thu., Sat.-Sun. 10am-6pm, Fri. 11am-6pm. Entry charge.

This museum, which is housed in the beautiful setting of the old flower market, traces the history of London's public transport system. Make sure you sit in the

The old flower market halls have been restored, and although Covent Garden has lost some of its authentic feel, the Piazza and Market are full of life and street entertainers. The restoration of the Royal Opera House and old Floral Hall have added a touch of class, and the old alleyways and courtyards, such as Neal's Yard, have had a makeover too. The old warehouses provide loft apartments for rich city whizz-kids. The shops around the pedestrianised Piazza sell street or sports fashion and this is still one of the nicest places to do your shopping.

driver's seat of a tube train or old-style routemaster bus. If you go with children, they'll love the interactive videos, and in the shop on the way out you'll find lots of fun gifts to take home with you.

❷ The Royal Opera House★★★

Bow St., WC2
☎ 020 7304 4000.
www.royalopera.org.uk.

Mahler conducted Wagner in this building, which dates from 1858. By extensive refurbishment and renovation, it has been transformed from an antiquated 19th-century

❹ Dr Marten's Store★★★
1-4 King's St., WC2
☎ **020 7497 1460**
Mon.-Sat. 9.30am-7pm,
Sun. noon-6pm.

If you think of Doc Marten's as clumpy boots worn only by young women dressed in black or young men with shaven heads, a visit to this shop will prove a real eye-opener. There are styles in every possible colour, some in leather, some in velvet and some smothered in flowers. As well as boots and shoes, you'll find sandals and jeans to go with your choice of footwear. There's a hairdresser to help you complete your look and a café that serves as a welcome refuge from the crowded streets outside, where you can recover from your bout of shopping.

theatre into a state-of-the-art 21st-century opera house. Its orchestra and the Royal Ballet company are world-famous.

❸ The Market★★★
Shops Mon.-Sat.
10am-6pm.
The two floors of the former fruit and vegetable market are filled with cafés, shops and stalls, while musicians and performers add to the atmosphere with open-air shows. Don't miss The Museum Store, 37 The Market ☎ 020 7431 7156, which sells copies of objects from museums all over the world, or Benjamin Pollock's wonderful toy shop, 44 Central Market (above Hobbs) ☎ 020 7379 7866.

❺ Buffalo★★
47-49 Neal St., WC2
☎ **020 7379 1051**
Mon.-Sat. 10.30am-7pm,
Sun. 2-6pm.

Buffalo was the original brand of platform shoes, subsequently copied by Morgan and No Name. Although some of them have soles up to 6 in/15 cm thick, they're so well designed they're both light and stable. Truly cool footwear. However, being up there with the fashion-conscious is going to cost you; some of the more outrageous styles are over £100.

❻ Food for Thought★
31 Neal St., WC2
☎ **020 7836 02 39**
Mon.-Sat. 9.30am-9pm.

This trendy vegetarian café-restaurant is a mecca for

organic food fans. You sit squashed together, but there are also alcove tables for more private conversations. The menu includes soup, pâté and salad washed down with carrot juice. An inexpensive way to do both your body and the environment a favour (around £7 a head).

❼ THE BOX
32-34 Monmouth St., WC2
☎ 020 7240 5828.

This trendy bar draws a very mixed crowd during the day, but is predominantly gay in the evening. It's a really friendly place, so make sure you take time out from your busy schedule to sit down at one of its pale wooden tables and soak up the calm, relaxed atmosphere. Besides, it's the perfect place to catch up on all the latest trends.

❽ The Loft★
35 Monmouth St., WC2
☎ 020 7240 3807
Mon.-Sat. 11am-6pm,
Sun. 1-5pm.

Fancy a Paul Smith suit, a Vivienne Westwood creation, or just an unusual sweater but can't afford to buy one? No problem! The ground floor is crammed with tempting and affordable menswear, while

in the basement ladies can find thet little black dress they spotted in their favourite magazine. Perfect dressing for the ideal couple.

❾ Cenci★★
31 Monmouth St., WC2
☎ 020 7836 14 00
Mon.-Sat. 11am-6.30pm.

Sweaters, suits, glasses, shirts, shoes, bags – the works. In other words, everything that could ever have been worn by your parents and grandparents and that you never thought to hang on to, when in fact it would have suited you down to the ground. A lovely shop, but a bit pricey for secondhand stuff.

❿ Black Out II★★
51 Endell St., WC2
☎ 020 7240 50 06
Mon.-Fri. 11am-7pm,
Sat. 11.30am-6.30pm.

One of London's finest shops for retro clothing. The stock ranges from

the Roaring Twenties to the Disco Years, via the spangled gowns of Hollywood stars and shirts printed for cousins of the Beach Boys. It's worth taking time and picking through the rails for the one bargain that will make your trip worthwhile.

⓫ Koh Samoui★★
65 Monmouth St., WC2
☎ 020 7240 4280
Mon.-Wed. and Sat.
11am-7pm., Thu.-Fri.
10am-7pm.

Wood, steel, dried flowers and the indispensable mirrors combine harmoniously in this shop, which has become a trail-blazing, style-creating outlet for young British fashion designers. Have no fear, you'll never see any of your colleagues coming to work in the skirt or blouse you've just bought for £75 or so

– all the designs are original and pretty well unique.

⑫ Screen Face★★
48 Monmouth St., WC2
☎ 020 7836 39 55
Mon.-Sat. 10am-7pm, Sun. noon–5pm.

Professional make-up from floor to ceiling, from simple mascara to false eyelashes for the stars of stage and screen. You'll also find products for body-painting – if you have ever fantasised about painting yourself gold all over! Prices are very reasonable and you can take the advice of the sales staff with confidence as they all work for theatre companies.

⑭ The Tea House★★★
15A Neal St., WC2
☎ 020 7240 7539
Mon.-Sat. 10am-7pm, Sun. noon-6pm.

The façade and interior of red and black laquered wood invite you to take a trip around the teapots. It may be

a fantasy journey, but it's high quality all the same, since in this shop you can explore the thousand-and-one faces of tea worship. The wonderful range of house teas includes every conceivable variety, including whisky-flavoured tea at £1.70 for 125 g/3¹⁄₂ oz. Make sure you have a look at the extraordinary teapot collection with pots of every shape and kind.

⑭ Neal's Yard Dairy★★★
17 Shorts Gardens, WC2
☎ 020 7379 7646
Mon.-Sat. 9am-7pm, Sun. 10am-5pm.

Neal's Yard has been part of the renaissance of English cheese. The ones on sale here are all either British or Irish, sometimes from isolated farms identifiable by the name stamped on the rind. They're made from cow's, goat's or ewe's milk, which is often unpasteurised. The owners, who opened the shop in 1979, give you enthusiastic advice and encourage you to taste before you buy. A real paradise for cheese-lovers.

Neal's Yard mural.

Around Carnaby Street
Centre of fashion

Oxford Circus

OXFORD CIRCUS

Oxford Street

Argyll St.

Little Argyll St.

Regent St.

Great Marlborough St.

Gr. Marlb. Pl.

Foubert's Pl.

Newburgh St.

Marshall St.

Kingly St.

Carnaby St.

Ganton St.

Broadwick Street

Beak St.

John St.

U. James St.

Golden Sq.

L. James St.

L. John St.

L. Brewer St.

Glasshouse St.

Poland Street

Noel St.

D'Arblay St.

Berwick St.

Wardour St.

Hopkins St.

Lexington St.

St.

Peter St.

Sherwood St.

3 · **2** · **8** · **11** · **7** · **5** · **4** · **10** · **12** · **14** · **1** · **6** · **13**

This part of Soho is one of London's fashion centres, where new designers open shops alongside well-known names. An ideal place to stock up on all that's hip and trendy without wearing yourself out.

❸ Laura Ashley★★
256-258 Regent St., SW1
☎ **020 7437 9760**

WELCOME TO CARNABY STREET

❶ Carnaby Street★★
This mythical street is where the 1960s trends were set, back in the days of flower-power, when the Beatles and the Rolling Stones used to fight over the number one spot in the Hit Parade. It was at the centre of Swinging London and the hippy movement. Today it's very touristy but still trendy.

❷ Berwick Street★
In an area crowded with tiny streets teaming with independent television and video companies, cutting rooms and sound studios, Berwick Street is the local shopping area. The street market offers everything from good, cheap fruit and vegetables to tacky tourist trinkets. Soho Silks (24 Berwick Street ☎ 020 7434 3305), is one of four shops that sell cloth made for some of the international fashion houses, at a fraction of the price of Liberty's. Little wonder that the costume-makers for the West End shows buy their fabrics here.

Mon.-Tues. 10am–6.30pm,
Wed., Fri. 10am–7pm, Thu.
10am–8pm, Sat 9.30-7pm,
Sun. noon-6pm.

This is just the shop for young
ladies of a romantic turn or
those who like their clothes
to match their gardens. The
styles are restrained and tend
towards the staid, while the
childrenswear tends towards
the neat and tidy - not to be
worn if painting or playing in
the sandpit.

❹ Liberty★★★
210-220 Regent St., W1
☎ **020 7734 1234**
Mon., Tue., Wed.
10am–6.30pm,
Thu. 10am–8pm
Fri–.Sat.
10am–7pm.

Liberty's
traditional fabrics
are decorated with
pretty flowers, but it's
much more than just a
fabric shop, although some
of them are very luxurious.
There are elegant women's
fashions and crockery too.
You'll find all
this famous
store's

traditions preserved within
its magnificent beamed and
wood-panelled interior.
You can also admire the

half-timbered
mock-Tudor façade on
Great Marlborough Street.

❺ Muji★★★
26 Great Marlborough St., W1
☎ **020 7287 7323**
Mon.-Sat. 10am–7pm, Thu.
10am-7.30pm Sun. noon-
6pm.

Unmissable! This shop's
interior design, pale wood
shelves and stands, reflects its
stock of stationery and articles
and accessories for the home,
all of which are characterised
by minimalist design and the
use of recycled paper. For just
a few pounds you can buy
yourself a pen that your boss
will drool over or a soap dish
that will give your bathroom a
touch of class. In other words,
unique items of matchless
design. The kind of shop that
keeps London at the cutting
edge of style.

❻ Hamleys★★
188-196 Regent St., W1
☎ **020 7494 2000**
Mon.-Wed. 10am-6.30pm,
Thu. 10am-8pm, Fri. 10am-
7pm Sat. 9.30am–7pm, Sun.
noon-6pm.

Even if you have no children,
don't miss out on a little
excursion into this enormous
toyshop, whose truly vast
array of wares of different
kinds makes it a
real tourist
attraction.
Confirmed toy
enthusiasts will
also want to check
out the Warner
Bros Store
at nos.
178-182
(☎ 020
7434 3334,
Mon.-Wed
and Fri.10am-
7pm, Tue.-Sat. 10am-8pm,
Sun. noon-6pm) and the
Disney Store at no. 140
(☎ 020 7287 6558, Mon.-Sat.
9.30am-8pm, Sun. noon-8pm).

❼ Agent Provocateur★★★
6 Broadwick St., W1
☎ **020 7439 0229**
Mon.-Sat. 11am-7pm.

So you've always fancied
yourself as a pin-up, but never

but you'll also find John Smedley knitwear and Patrick Cox shoes. Very colourful, very trendy, very London.

⑩ Jess James★★
3 Newburgh St., W1
☎ 020 7437 0199
Mon.-Fri. 11am-6.30pm,
Thu. 11am-7pm,
Sat. 11am-6pm.

Set off the clothes you've just bought at Dispensary with a similarly futuristic ring or bracelet from this shop with its wonderful window displays. No question – one trip to Newburgh Street and everyone will assume you're an avid reader of *Dazed and Confused* (see p. 107).

⑪ Vexed Generation★★
3 Berwick St., W1
☎ 020 7287 6224
Mon.-Sat. 11.30am-6.30pm.

found the right accessories? Then Agent Provocateur will satisfy your every desire. In its boudoir-like interior, you're bound to find just the bra to bring out the sex-kitten in you.

⑧ Yo! Sushi★★
52 Poland St., W1
☎ 020 7287 0443
Every day, 12 noon-11pm.

Never mind that the sushi isn't terribly authentic, this restaurant takes the cyber-diner concept to its limits.

You sit at a high-tech counter, grabbing the food items that take your fancy as they glide past on a conveyor belt. The colour of the plate represents the price of your dish. Drinks are brought to you by R2D2's baby brother. Additional atmosphere is provided by three screens showing continuous MTV, so forget any private conversation unless you're both good lip-readers.

⑨ Dispensary★★
9 and 15 Newburgh St., W1
☎ 020 7287 8145
Mon.-Sat. 10.30am-6.30pm.

Two shops in the same street, one for men and one for women. Dispensary label designs are particularly good (beautiful sweaters from £59),

Whether you're an Internet surfer, a cyberpunk or just can't wait to see how fashion's going to develop in the third millennium, don't forget to call in here, where you may come across a fashion writer interviewing the designer who created these garments. They're straight out of *2001 A Space Odyssey*. Don't miss this new and truly exciting, very London shop.

⓬ Contemporary Ceramics★
7 Marshall St., W1
☎ **020 7437 7605.**
Mon.-Sat. 10am-5.30pm,
Thu. 10am–7pm.

This is the shop window of British craft potters, both metaphorically and literally, since all the wares on sale are on display in the bay windows, from crockery and vases to jewellery. Many of the pieces are one-offs, but prices are very reasonable.

⓭ Aquascutum★★
100 Regent St., W1
☎ **020 7675 8200**
Mon.-Sat. 10am-6.30pm,
Thu. 10am-7pm,
Sun noon-5pm.

Traditionally smart British elegance predominates in this large store selling fashions for men and women in a pale, rather impersonal interior. You won't find anything revolutionary here and the customers tend to be middle-aged, but the sales assistants are pleasant and it's an excellent place to buy a mac.

⓮ Simply Sausages★
93 Berwick St., W1
☎ **020 7287 3482**
Mon.-Fri. 8am-6pm,
Sat. 9.30am-4.30pm.

The window is full of different coloured sausages – green ones with spinach, curry-

flavoured yellow ones, red ones full of chilli, black puddings and many more. Vegetarians are catered for, as

well as meat-eaters, and many of the sausages are guaranteed pork-free. One of London's most interesting markets, busy, cheap Berwick St, is in full swing outside.

If you want to walk around a little longer, or you're interested in tableware, make sure you go right the way down Regent St. Besides the shops selling clothes and toys already mentioned, you'll find many selling china, including **Chinacraft** at no. 134 (☎ 020 7434 2502). Their mid-January and mid-June china sales have knock-down prices. Downstairs is a branch of the **Reject China Shop,** with cut-price goods. Also worth checking out are **Royal Doulton** at no. 154 (☎ 020 7734 3184), and the silverware at **Kings of Sheffield**, no. 319 (☎ 020 7637 9888). A great way to buy several items that go together without having to spend all day over it.

Around Old Compton Street
Epicentre of Gay London

In the last few years, Old Compton Street has reinvented itself as the trendy centre of outrageous style in London. The gay community congregates in the bars and pubs along the street. It's the place to check out what's hot, what's cool and where your next party's coming from in its many bars or read Boyz, the gay London free sheet. You can observe the continual and transitory rebirth of London's avant-garde here. The show just goes on and on, so find a table, settle down and watch the world go by. This is also where you can buy the best coffee and tea in town.

❶ The Palace Theatre★
Shaftesbury Ave., W1
☎ 020 7434 0909.

This is one of the six theatres to be found on Shaftesbury Avenue. The street is almost entirely devoted to shows of one kind or another, and boasts two cinemas as well. Of them all the Palace Theatre has the most interesting façade. You can only visit its luxurious interior during performances.

❷ Soho Square★

Get your breath back in this lovely garden, with its charming little mock-Tudor house built in the Victorian period. For a long time, this square was a very exclusive place. Take a look at the 17th-century residence at no. 10, for example, which reflects the area's former splendour. Beatlemaniacs can pay hommage in front of Paul McCartney's former office at no. 2.

❸ Clone Zone★★

64 Old Compton St., W1
☎ 020 7287 3530
Mon.-Sat.
11am-9pm,
Sun 1-7pm.

Everything
for the gay
life-style.
On one
floor hot
fashion,
gadgets, pens, mugs, watches
and the essentials to read or
listen to. And on the second
floor, items for more exotic
and adventurous pastimes.

❹ American Retro★★

35 Old Compton St. W1
☎ 020 7734 3477
Mon.-Fri. 10.30am-7.30pm.
Sat. 10am–7pm.

THE BEST CAFÉS IN THE AREA.

The **Old Compton Café**, at no. 34, is
frequented by gays. The
terrace is very busy, and it's
open 24 hours a day. The
Balans, at no. 60, is only
slightly more mixed. The
Freedom, nearby at no.
60 Wardour St., is one of
the most fashionable of all.
Anyone nostalgic for New
York's yuppie bars will love
the **Mezzo**, at no. 100,
which is a perfect example
of its kind.

A shop selling unusual
accessories for gays and
fashion-victims. On the
ground floor, you'll find hip
clothes for men (Belgian
techno-designer W&LT), wild
jewellery, postcards and art
books, while in the basement
there are colourful and fun
items for the home. Loads of
original gift ideas.

❺ Kokon to Zai★★★

57 Greek St., W1
☎ 020 7434 13 16
Mon.-Sat. 11am-8.30pm.

This shop may be small,
but it's an international
trendsetter, with limited
editions of house music discs,
the latest Nike trainers
imported direct from the USA,
and clothes by European and
Japanese designers who'll be
famous next year or perhaps
the year after. The stock
changes faster than fashion.
It's what you want to be seen in,
but it doesn't come cheap.

❻ Algerian Coffee Stores★★

52 Old Compton St., W1
☎ 020 7437 2480
Mon.-Sat. 9am-7pm.

The window is a muddle of
teapots, coffee-pots, and

packets of tea and coffee, and
inside the old-fashioned shop
is as much of a jumble, with
all sorts of wares on display.
This is where you can buy the
best tea and coffee in London.

❼ Pâtisserie Valérie★★★

44 Old Compton St., W1
☎ 020 7437 3466
Mon.-Sat. 7.30am-10pm.
Sun. 9.30am–7pm.

A haven of sense and good
taste which almost feels out of
place in the pounding energy
and excess of Old Compton St.
This is one of the best places
to stop for an excellent French
pastry and a large cappuccino.

❽ Milroy's Soho Wine Market★★

3 Greek St., W1
☎ 020 7437 9311
Mon.-Fri. 11am-11pm,

Here you'll find every whisky
imaginable. The
sales assistants
are very good
at explaining
the subtle
differences
between
the
hundreds
of brands
they have
on offer.

Around the British Museum

The British Museum, dominating this corner of Bloomsbury, has long been a favourite haunt of London's intellectuals, such as Virginia Woolf and T.S. Eliot. The contents of the famous Reading Room have been temporarily rehoused in the British Library while building work is completed. The University of London is also here, so you'll see lots of earnest people studying for exams while you contemplate the scenery.

❶ British Museum★★★
Great Russell St., WC1
☎ 020 7323 8299
www.british-museum.ac.uk
Mon.-Sat. 10am-5pm, Sun. noon-6pm.
Entry free.

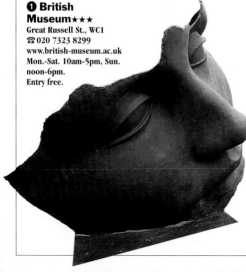

Make time for the British Museum, which has more visitors than the Louvre in Paris or the Metropolitan Museum in New York. You must see the Rosetta Stone, which was the key to deciphering Egyptian hieroglyphs – it's near the

entrance. Head for the Egyptian collection and the Elgin marbles from the Parthenon, which Greece is still trying to get back. A major redevelopment focussed round the Reading Room and Great Court is under construction. The inner court will be a dramatic new space that will be open to the public for the first time in 150 years.

❷ Bedford Square★★

All the entrances on this very fine Georgian square (1775) are decorated with artificial stone. Did you know that this area is one of the many private estates that combine to make up London? Though some parts of the city belong to the Crown, the area in which you're now standing belongs to the Duke of Bedford.

❸ Russell Square★★

From a bench in this garden, you can admire some of the city's loveliest Victorian houses.

❹ St George's Bloomsbury★

Bloomsbury Way, WC1
☎ 020 7405 3044
Mon.-Fri. 9.30am-5.30pm.
Mass Wed., Fri. 1.10pm
Sung eucharist Sun. 10.30am.

This church, designed by Nicholas Hawksmoor for the district's rich inhabitants, has always been the subject of criticism and mockery. Its fake Renaissance northern façade, pyramid bell-tower resembling a mausoleum and highly unpopular statue of King George I may have something to do with this.

❺ Westaway and Westaway★★

65 Great Russell St., WC1
☎ 020 7405 4479
Mon.-Sat. 9am-5.30pm,
Sun. 10.30am-5.30pm.

This shop smells slightly of mothballs, and is a far cry from Dr Marten's. However, if you're buying woollens and tartans for the whole family, you'll get the best possible value for money. There's less choice than elsewhere and the colours can be a bit unimaginative, but the Shetland knits won't wear out so quickly.

❻ James Smith & Sons★★★

53 New Oxford St., WC1
☎ 020 7836 4731
Mon.-Fri. 9.30am-5.30pm,
Sat. 10am-5.30pm.

Smith & Sons is simply the best umbrella shop you could possibly imagine. The interior dates from 1857 and displays thousands of umbrellas to put a smile on your face when skies are grey. Even if you don't need a brolly, have

❼ PIED BULL YARD
A charming alleyway between Bloomsbury Square and Bury Place with a cluster of camera shops (a speciality of the area), and **Truckles**, a friendly café where they put tables outside in summer. The line of antiquarian booksellers along nearby Museum Street may remind you that Charles Dickens, Virginia Woolf and T. S. Eliot all lived round here.

a look at the traditional swordsticks and the more unusual umbrellas that open automatically.

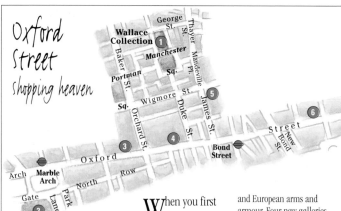

Oxford Street shopping heaven

Wallace Collection ①
George St.
Thayer St.
Baker St.
Manchester
Portman St.
Manchester Sq.
Mandeville Pl.
Wigmore St.
James St. ⑤
Portman Sq.
Orchard St.
Duke St.
⑥
Street
③
④
Bond St.
New Bond St.
Oxford
Street
Bond Street
Arch
Marble Arch
North Row
Gate
Park Lane
②

When you first come out onto Oxford Street, it feels as though the rest of the world is already here. Though the pavements are very wide, they're often overflowing with crowds pouring in and out of the shops and department stores. But don't let the hustle and bustle overwhelm you – this is the heart of shopper's London. A bit of friendly advice: the smaller side streets, like St Christopher's Place, tend to be much quieter, and many of them have nice little cafés where you can sit down and get your strength and spirits back.

❶ Wallace Collection ★★★

Herford House, Manchester Square, W1
☎ **020 7935 0687**
(also for disabled access)
Mon.-Sat. 10am-5pm, Sun. 2-5pm. Entry free.

Leave the frenzied consumerism of Oxford Street behind and step inside what was once the private residence of the well-known art collector, Sir Richard Wallace. His entire collection of European paintings was left to the nation – miniatures and sculpture, French 18th-century furniture, porcelain, golsdmiths' work and oriental and European arms and armour. Four new galleries are opening in mid-2000 to mark the centenary of the opening of the collection.

❷ Speaker's Corner ★★

Hyde Park, Sun. afternoons.

You can witness one of the most extraordinary of London's many traditions in action on the corner of Hyde Park, opposite Marble Arch. Every Sunday since 1872 speakers have been competing for the attention of passers-by. Anybody can speak on any subject they choose. Don't miss the chance to see democracy at work.

❸ Marks & Spencer ★

458 Oxford St., W1
☎ **020 7935 7954**
Mon.-Sat. 9am-8pm, Sat. 9am-7pm, Sun. noon-6pm.

There are Marks & Spencer's stores all over London. The clothes on sale inside aren't expensive and the quality is generally good, particularly the underwear and woollens. There's also a range of gifts and toiletries, as well as some well-made home furnishings. The food department is excellent, with a wide range of products at reasonable prices. A brand you can depend on.

❹ Selfridges★★
400 Oxford St., W1
☎ **020 7629 1234**
Mon.-Wed. 10am-7pm, Thu.-Fri. 10am-8pm, Sat. 9.30am-7pm, Sun. noon-6pm.

Though it's suffered from a reputation of being the poor man's Harrods, it's worth making the effort to visit Selfridges. The store is in a superb Art Nouveau building and offers a fine range of products, and fashion from street style to designer labels.

The vast perfume hall stocks all the major brands of toiletries and make-up, and you can have free makeovers and consult the experts. They also have stylish linens and household goods. A great place for a browse (especially if it's raining!).

❺ St Christopher's Place★★★
This is one of the prettiest pedestrianised areas in London, with a great many different shops. Whistles, at nos. 20-21, sells clothes by

some very gifted young designers (such as Sonja Nuttal) at very affordable prices. Buckle My Shoe, at

no. 19, has the widest selection of children's shoes in London (see p. 90).

❻ John Lewis★
278-306 Oxford St., W1
☎ **020 7629 7711**
Mon.-Fri. 9am-6pm, Sat. 9.30am-6pm, Thu. 10am-8pm.

The haberdashery department at John Lewis is famous throughout London. You'll find everything you could possibly need here to make your own clothes or give your wardrobe a makeover. The store is famous for its quality and unbeatable prices. And these days you can pay with a credit card, too.

> ## BUCKINGHAM PALACE IN A SNOWSTORM
>
> Along Oxford Street there are stalls selling souvenirs. The range is as wide as any you'll find in a shop, so you could treat yourself to a teapot shaped like a London bus or Buckingham Palace in a snowstorm. But some stalls sell fakes – be on the alert.

Mayfair Designer clothes and antiques

❶ Sotheby's★★
34-35 New Bond St., W1
☎ **020 7293 5000**
**Mon.-Fri. 9am-4.30pm,
some Sun. 12-4pm for
exceptional sales (phone
to book).**

This is the oldest auction house in London (1744), and the main competitor of the other auction house, Christie's. Exhibitions of the lots to be sold go on show to the public (catalogues are also made available). Have a look at the Egyptian statue of the goddess Sekhmet, which dates from 1320 BC. You can also have lunch in Sotheby's stylish café in the entrance.

Mayfair has been an exclusive area since the 18th century and this is where you find real luxury goods. It's the home of establishments dealing in works of art, such as the highly respectable Colnaghi's, and Sotheby's auction house, though unfortunately these institutions are closed on Saturdays. Old and New Bond Street form the heart of this walk. Also wander down South Molton Street, which is for pedestrians only, and is lined with shoe shops and designer boutiques. There's even a designer nail bar.

❷ St George's, Hanover Square★★★
St George St.

This church is regarded as the finest in the West End and is one of the earliest examples of Georgian architecture. It was built in 1724 and played host to the composer Handel and the weddings of famous British writers Shelley (in 1814) and George Elliot (in 1880). It's worth going inside to see the stained-glass windows and George I's coat of arms.

❸ Berkeley Square★
This square is surrounded by beautiful 18th-century residences. Particularly

worth seeing is no. 44, on the corner of Hay Hill. It was built in 1744 and its magnificent interior makes it one of the finest private houses in London. When the lights are on at night, you can see the wonderful ceiling in the main drawing-room, which is blue and gold.

❹ Nicole Farhi★★
158 New Bond St., W1
☎ 020 7499 8368
Mon.-Sat. 10am-6.30pm.
Thu. 10am-7pm.

Nicole Farhi's flagship shop combines fashion with comfort in her classically-styled, high-quality clothing. Busy professional women greatly appreciate the practical elegance of her suits. There's also a restaurant in this shop, which has become extremely popular.

❺ Vivienne Westwood Red Label★★★
44 Conduit St., W1
☎ 020 7439 1109
Mon.-Sat. 10.30am-6pm.
Thu. 10am-7pm.

The most recent of Westwood's shops, and her second line, Red Label, reflect the iconoclastic exuberance of the high priestess of punk. There are suits with provocatively plunging necklines and bustles (£300-400), twin-sets for men (£150) and spangly skulls to wear as pendants or cufflinks. Definitely worth a visit just for the experience.

❻ Smythson★★
44 New Bond St., W1
☎ 020 7629 8558
Mon.-Fri. 9.30am-6pm, Sat. 10am-5.30pm.

The most 'classy' stationers in London, with extremely pleasant sales staff, which, strangely, is not always the norm around here. You don't have to be a millionaire to treat yourself and the writing paper is wonderful.

❼ Bond Street Antique Centre★★
124 New Bond St., W1
☎ 020 7351 53 53
Mon.-Fri. 10am-5.45pm, Sat. 11am-5.30pm.

This ultra-chic gallery has shops specialising in period jewellery and silverware, but you can also find good china here. Every piece is exceptional, with prices to match. A very prestigious place to buy from, but you could equally well pay a visit just to dream.

❽ Church's★★★
133 New Bond St., W1
☎ 020 7493 1474
Mon.-Sat. 9am-6.30pm, Thu. 9am-7pm.

Every man with a yen for classical footware has to call in at Church's Bond St. store. The range is much wider than in branches elsewhere and the prices are lower.

Church's also make a range of styles of equally fine quality for women. Women's prices start at aroud £90, while it's twice that for men. However, it's a statistically proven fact that men wear their shoes out less quickly …

❾ Asprey and Garrard★★★
165-169 New Bond St., W1
☎ 020 7493 6767.
Mon.-Fri. 10am-6pm,
Sat. 10am-5pm.

Asprey and Garrard is the amalgamation of two great names, both with a reputation for fine craftsmanship, brought together in one shop. Garrard, the Crown Jewellers, display their exquisite jewellery in this British temple to interior design, and on the first floor is Asprey's collection of English furniture from the 17th and 18th centuries, worthy of any museum of decorative arts. There's a lovely selection of china and the prices are no higher than elsewhere.

❿ DKNY★★
27 Old Bond St., W1
☎ 020 7499 8089
Mon.-Wed. 10am-6pm, Thu. 10am-7pm, Fri. 10am-6pm, Sat. 10am-6.30pm.

The store design is amazing and the New York designer, Donna Karan cuts clothes for women with an eye to comfort. The lifts look like something out of a science fiction film and the patrons in the café by the entrance could have walked off the set of *Absolutely fabulous*. Pleasant, easy-going sales staff.

⓫ Jigsaw★
126 New Bond St., W1
☎ 020 7491 4484
Mon.-Sat. 10am-6.30pm,
Thu. 10am-7pm.

Jigsaw is a franchised brand selling good-quality clothes cut to original designs for all the family. This is a magnificent store and it acts to some extent as the label's shop window. The space is attractively presented and the range is as wide as you would expect to find in the luxury shops in the neighbourhood, but the prices are generally much more affordable.

⓬ Paul Smith★★★
23 Avery Row, W1
☎ 020 7493 1287
Mon.-Sat. 10am-6pm,
Thu. 10am-7pm.

The last two seasons' collections for men are on sale here with minimum reductions of between 30 and 50%. Jeans start at £19, trousers at £30, and you may get a suit for £300, in other words half the normal price. A great shop, which still isn't very well known.

⓭ Browns★★
**18, 23-27, 38, 50 and 62
South Molton St., W1**
☎ 020 7491 7833.

If Browns had bought up
South Molton St. in its entirety,
things wouldn't be much
different, as it already occupies
almost one in two of the
street's shops. It sells designer
collections (Jil Sander, Romeo
Gigli, etc.), as well as its own
line at no. 50. Don't miss the
great reductions on the first
floor of no. 38.

⓮ Claridge's★★★
Brook St., W1
☎ 020 7629 8860.

Make a point of having tea
here – the cakes are delicious.
It's served in the foyer every
day 3-5.30pm, and is rather a

formal affair. They don't like
jeans and expect men to wear
a tie. It's a good idea to book
in advance, too.

⓯ The Guinea Grill★
30 Bruton Pl., W1
☎ 020 7499 1210
**Mon.-Fri. lunch 12.30-
2.30pm, Mon.-Sat. evening
6.30- 11pm.**

This is absolutely the best
place in London to sample
steak and kidney pie, though
you'd better make sure you
get here early as the
restaurant is extremely
popular and gets full. But
don't panic if you arrive too
late and the house speciality
is all gone, you'll still have
a selection of traditional

English specialities to choose
from, and you'll enjoy a
delicious meal. Here's a tip,
if you go at lunchtime, the
prices are cheaper.

A FACE THAT FITS

The shops in this area
are among the most
luxurious in London, or
indeed the world, and they
enjoy the privilege of
supplying London's gentry.
You should just be aware
that, as a result, you may
come across sales staff
who are a little formal
and sometimes off-putting.
However, forewarned is
forearmed, so don't let
yourself be intimidated.

A walk in the City from the Tower of London to St Paul's Cathedral

The City is still very much a man's world, though times are changing. The booming Square Mile is full of buzzing, energetic bars and restaurants teeming with exuberant brokers, traders, stockbrokers, bankers and financiers who deal in millions. An evening drink in a couple of bars or pubs will give you more insight into City life than any organised tour. Beside the gleaming modern buildings, there's a warren of ancient streets, St Paul's and the Tower. But it's only worth doing this walk on a weekday.

❶ Tower of London★★★
Tower Hill, EC3
☎ 020 7709 0765
www.hrp.org.uk
Nov.-Feb Tue.-Sat.
9am- 4pm, Sun. 10am-4pm,
Mar.-Oct. Mon.-Sat. 9am-
5pm, Sun. 10am-5pm.

Entry charge, disabled access.

As you come out of the tube station, the Tower rises before you like an impregnable fortress. It was built in 1097 to protect London from potential invaders. When none showed up, it was used as a royal residence and, most notably, as a prison. Shivers are guaranteed in the Martin Tower, where instruments of torture are exhibited.

❷ St Paul's Cathedral★★★
Ludgate Hill, EC4
☎ 020 7236 4128
Mon.-Sat. 8.30am-4pm,
Sunday services 11.30am
(Sung Eucharist), and 6pm
(Evensong). Entry charge.

When the original St Paul's was destroyed in the Great Fire of London in 1666, Sir Christopher Wren was commissioned to rebuild it. He turned for inspiration to St Peter's in Rome. Climb up to the Whispering Gallery, where the sound of your voice carries to the other side of the dome.

Then cross the river over the new Millennium Bridge.

❸ Mansion House
☎ 020 7626 2500
(pre-booked group visits, Tue.-Thu. only)

and St Stephen's Walbrook★★
Walbrook, EC4.

The Mansion House is the official residence of the Lord Mayor of London. Take a look at its neo-Palladian façade and magnificent pseudo-Egyptian hall with fluted pillars. To the left of the Mansion House, you'll find the façade of **St Stephen's Walbrook** (39 Walbrook, EC4 ☎ 020 7626 8284, Mon.-Thu. 10am-4pm, Fri. 10am-3pm), one of the finest in the city, designed by Wren and completed in 1679.

❹ Leadenhall Market★★★
Whittington Av., EC3

Mon.-Fri. 7am-4pm.
There are still a few stalls selling food (particularly game and poultry) inside this superb Victorian market hall, which was built in 1881. However, cheap clothes sellers have moved in and all but taken over.

❺ Penhaligon's★★
8 Cornhill,
The Royal Exchange, EC3
☎ 020 7283 0711
Mon.-Fri. 10am-6pm.

This shop, in the shadow of the Royal Exchange, is a model of understated elegance. Its refined perfumes can be detected even in the corridors of Buckingham Palace. You can also buy Victorian-style vaporisers here and wonderful beauty accessories. Magnificent 30ml silver vaporisers from £155.

THE CROWN JEWELS
Same times as the Tower of London. Entry charge.

You can admire the jewels without exhausting yourself as a travelator has been installed to stop visitors spending too much time looking at them! Almost all the royal insignia were destroyed by Cromwell during the period of the Commonwealth (1649-1660), and the ones on show today in a room in the Tower mostly date from the coronation of Charles II in 1661, when the monarchy was restored. Don't miss Queen Elizabeth's crown or the enormous diamond in the royal sceptre.

❻ The Jamaica Wine House★★
St Michael's Alley, EC3
☎ 020 7626 9496
Mon.-Fri. 11.30am-8pm.

This was the first coffee house to open in London in 1652. From outside, it looks like a little museum, with its windows full of old bills and dusty bottles. But it maintains tradition, and no-one is allowed in without a tie. Frequented by insiders and regulars.

Knightsbridge *Department stores and exclusive shops*

Knightsbridge is a veritable haven for luxury shopping and gracious living. It's in the quieter streets that you'll find the finest treasures.

If you leave the lights of Harrods behind, you'll find smaller shops filled with endlessly tempting fashions and decorative items for the home. To get into the mood and remind yourself how clothes and interior design have changed over the years, you could pay a visit to the Victoria and Albert Museum which is just down the road.

❶ Victoria and Albert Museum★★★

Cromwell Rd, SW1
☎ 020 7938 8441
www.vam.ac.uk
Mon.-Sun. 10am-5.45pm
Entry charge.

This exceptional museum of decorative art is, without a doubt, one of the finest in the world. It houses objects from Europe and the former British colonies. If you're short of time, the one thing you must see out of all its treasures is the statue of 'The Three Graces' by Canova, which was recently acquired by the museum (check first though, as the statue spends six months of the year in Edinburgh). But if you've got a few hours, make sure you see the Nehru Gallery (16th-19th-century Indian art), the costume displays (17th-20th-century textiles) and the 20th-century furniture collection.

❷ The Scotch House★★

2 Brompton Rd, SW1
☎ 020 7581 2151
Mon.-Tue., Thu.-Fri., 9.30am-6pm, Wed. 10am-7pm, Sun. 12-6pm.

Almost 250 different tartans are on display in the enormous room at the centre of this shop. From woollen scarves to cashmere jumpers you'll find a selection including every imaginable style (V- and turtle-neck jumpers, twin-sets etc), colour and yarn you could wish for.

Look at the window displays for a free intensive course in fashion, then step inside for the practical. There's a selection of designer labels and ready-to-wear ranges. 'Harvey Nicks' is about quality. There's also a restaurant and a bar on the fifth floor, a sushi counter and a luxurious food hall.

❻ M P Levene★★
5 Thurloe Pl., SW7
☎ 020 7589 3744
Mon.-Fri. 9am-6pm,
Sat 9am-1pm.

A sumptuous selection of English silverware, centrepieces and candelabra, both secondhand and antique. Levene's will also make you a silver replica of your yacht! They also carry a selection of 250 different designs of cuff links.

❸ Harrods★★★
87-135 Brompton Rd, SW1
☎ 020 7730 1234
Mon.-Tue., Thu.-Fri. 9.30am-6pm, Wed. 10am-7pm, Sat 9am-6pm, Sun. noon-6pm.

you start? With so many departments housed on the store's five floors, you're spoilt for choice.

You can't possibly leave Knightsbridge without one of those famous green and gold bags. Make sure you buy at least a teddy bear – Harrods sells the finest traditional bears. And you definitely mustn't miss the celebrated Food Hall, with its vast range and wonderful displays. As for all the other things, where do

❹ Pandora
★★★
16-22 Cheval Pl., SW7
☎ 020 7589 5289
Mon.-Sat. 9am-6pm.

Pandora sells second hand clothes from major designers in very good condition. All are classic styles in impeccable taste, and the coats are terrific. Best of all you can feel and try things on without getting disdainful looks. The small streets nearby are worth a visit in themselves.

❺ Harvey Nichols★★★
109-125 Knightsbridge
☎ 020 7235 5000
Mon.-Tue. and Sat. 10am-7pm, Wed.-Fri 10am-8pm, Sun noon-6pm.

❼ BEAUCHAMP PLACE

This is one of the area's smartest and most fashionable streets. The designer Caroline Charles, at nos 56-57 (see p. 84), creates clothes for princesses. She can make you look like royalty, too but obviously at designer prices. The interior design is more like a private drawing-room than a clothes shop.

Chelsea Down the King's Road

Twenty years ago, hanging out on the King's Road was truly trendy. The first punks were glowering at the world from the shop of a certain Vivienne Westwood and the hip avant-gardists were changing attitudes in Chelsea and causing ructions further afield. But times have changed and fashion is happening elsewhere. The shops still keep up with the latest trends, but success has turned the King's Road sleek and smart. It's still lovely for a pleasant walk though, and popular with Londoners for their Saturday afternoon shopping trips.

devoted to stylish furniture, fabrics and articles for the home.

❷ The Pheasantry★★
152 King's Rd, SW3.

Stop for a few moments to admire the façade of this restaurant. It was originally built in 1765, but was transformed by a French family in 1881. The front door is an imitation of the Arc de Triomphe in Paris. Before becoming a restaurant, the building was home to the ballet school where Dame Margot Fonteyn did her first *pliés*.

❸ Steinberg and Tolkien★★★
193 King's Rd, SW3
☎ 020 7376 3660
Mon.-Sat. 10.30am-7pm,
Sun. noon-6.30pm.

Girls in the know shop here for unusual yet inexpensive items, from spangles, silk and satin to dresses, court shoes and evening bags in the best tradition of glamour and

❶ King's Road★★★

After falling out of favour for a while, the King's Road has regained its attractive, busy air. It's a very popular spot with Londoners, has far fewer tourists than Covent Garden and more affordable prices than the shops in the exclusive areas of Mayfair and Knightsbridge. This former route of royalty is home to the finest child-orientated shops in town, such as **Daisy and Tom** (no. 181 ☎ 020 7352 5000) where you're bound to find plenty of ideas for successful gifts. Another address to remember is the branch of **Heal's** (no. 224, ☎ 020 7349 8411), a shop

glitz. It's a survivor of the King's Road's grand old days and has something for the most discerning customer.

❹ Mandy★★
139 King's Rd, SW3
☎ 020 7376 7491
Mon.-Sat. 10am-7pm
Sun. noon-6pm.

If you want to make an impression and dress at the cutting edge of fashion, you need only come here. With satin trousers in any colour you could wish for, and trendy little tops, this is the best clubwear shop in the whole of the King's Road.

The Bibendum building in Fulham Road (see p.76) is one of the most spectacular in Chelsea.

❺ World's End Vivienne Westwood★★★
430 King's Rd, SW3
☎ 020 7352 6551
Mon.-Sat. 9.30am-6pm.
Wed. 9,30am-7pm.

Vivienne Westwood and Malcom McLaren invented punk, but these days mohican hairstyles and safety-pins have been replaced by swarms of tourists. Westwood has become internationally known for her unique slant on fashion. This is her original shop, which now sells her Anglomania and Sportswear ranges.

> The Royal Borough of Brasington and Chelsea
> **ROYAL**
> **AVENUE.** **S.W.3**

❻ Royal Avenue ★
This avenue was created in the late 17th century for King William III, who wanted to link his new Kensington

residence to the Royal Hospital. It got no further than the King's Road. Ian Fleming made it famous by choosing it as the London address of James Bond.

❼ THE ROYAL HOSPITAL
The Royal Hospital, on Royal Avenue, was designed in 1682 by Sir Christopher Wren and is home to 400 old soldiers, or Chelsea Pensioners, who wear distinctive scarlet uniforms. In May, the Chelsea Flower show is held in the gardens.

A breath of air in Hampstead

Leave the noise and fury of central London behind and take a trip to Hampstead, a charming district with a village atmosphere that's especially popular on Sundays. It's an airy residential district with peaceful, elegant streets and attractive shops. The village atmosphere and magnificent heath bring a little of the country to the city. Hampstead is only a few tube stops from the centre and definitely worth a visit.

① HAMPSTEAD HEATH

East Heath

The Mount Hampstead Sq. **Cannon Pl.** **Christ Church** **Walk** **Road**

New End St. New End Sq. **Well** **Hill**

Street **Back Lane** **Flask Walk** **Willow Rd.** ③ **Willoughby Rd.**

Holly Hill ⑤

Hampstead ④ Perrin's Court ⑥ **Gayton Rd.**

Church Row ② **Fitzjohn's Avenue** Hampstead High St.

Hampstead, so do take a few steps down it, even though it's lined entirely with private houses, just to soak up its typically British atmosphere. And be sure to look at the magnificent wrought-iron gates at the front of each house.

① Hampstead Heath★★★
☎ 020 8455 5183
Open every day.

If you're a nature-lover, you'll adore this 80 hectare/200 acre park. It's a favourite spot for a Sunday afternoon walk and, if you're lucky enough to go to Hampstead in summer, you can swim in one of its open-air pools. The heath is much quieter and wilder than London's many other parks, and on a fine day it gives you an unbeatable view across the city.

② Church Row★★
Stop for a few moments to admire this Georgian street, which is one of the best preserved in London. It's also one of the prettiest in

Hampstead has several lively shopping streets. It's an excellent place to end up on your Sunday afternoon walk because of it's clutch of decent fashion shops, **Nicole Farhi**, **Karen Millen**, and **Next**, which, like most shops here, are open on Sundays. There are also some more unusual, individual shops to investigate.

❸ Flask Walk and Well Walk★★

These two streets are lined with small shops, including the **Humla Children's Shop** (☎ 020 7794 8449, Mon.-Sat. 10am-6pm, Sun. noon-6pm) at no. 10 Flask Walk, selling charming children's clothes, and, at no. 11, **The Garden Shop**, an ideal place to pause

if Hampstead's pastoral atmosphere has given you a yen to buy plants to take home. A few celebrities have lived in Well Walk, including the great English painter John Constable, at no. 40.

❹ Louis Pâtisserie★★★
32 Heath St., NW3
☎ 020 7435 9908
Mon.-Sun. 9am-6pm.

This café is generally packed, but queue up and wait for a table, then enjoy the most

delicious cakes imaginable made from the finest ingredients. You can buy them to take away, but it's much more fun to eat them at one of the café tables with the local cosmopolitan crowd.

❺ R.A.S (Ruth Aram Shop)★★
65 Heath St., Hampstead, NW3
☎ 020 7431 4008
Mon.-Sat. 10am-6pm, Sun. 11.30am-5.30pm.

This shop sells furniture and accessories for the home in fun designs. Even the most boring object looks new and different here, and you'll find the latest creations by the great British

designers Jasper Conran and Ron Arad. On the other side of the street there's a brand new glass-fronted shopping arcade full of upmarket clothes shops.

❻ Designer Second Hand Shop★★
24 Hampstead High St., NW3
☎ 020 7431 8618
Mon.-Sun. 11.30am-6pm.

Make sure you call in here to buy your designer clothes at truly unbeatable prices. It's a tiny shop and the shelves are groaning with all kinds of garments, so you'll have to search very patiently to find just the right outfit.

Rooms and restaurants Practicalities

HOTELS

You're more than likely to choose a hotel for the weekend because of its location. In a weekend you won't want to waste time travelling further than you have to, so it's better to stay somewhere in central London. British hotels tend to be comparatively expensive. Prices are usually given per room, single, twin or double, but be sure to check that prices quoted include all taxes, VAT, and service charges, otherwise you could be in for a nasty surprise when you get the final bill. Breakfast isn't usually included. There are often tea-making facilities in rooms, so after your morning cuppa, go off and have breakfast elsewhere. You're not expected to leave a tip, except in luxury hotels where you should tip the porter.

As well as the selection you'll find in this guide, the British Tourist Office has a choice of establishments classified in terms of the number of crowns they've been awarded that it might be useful for you to consult before you set off (see p. 9). You can also call the London Tourist Board's telephone accommodation booking service on ☎ 020 7604 2890 This will give you access to a great many hotels at a wide range of prices.

All the addresses given in this guide are located in the centre of the city and classified by area. It's important to bear in mind that there are enormous variations in hotel prices and that a high price doesn't automatically reflect high quality. Some hotels offer non-smoking rooms.

To book a room from home before you leave, which you're strongly advised to do, telephone the hotel of your choice to check room availablility for the dates you require, and confirm by fax or letter. You'll be asked to pay a deposit using a credit or debit card. All hotels accept major credit cards, such as Visa and Mastercard. If you want to book from outside the UK and don't have a credit card you can pay by bank draft or ask a hotel booking agency or travel agent to organise your stay.

You should aim to arrive at your hotel before 6pm to ensure that the room you've booked isn't given to another guest. If you're likely to arrive late, it's best to mention it when you book, so there'll be no problem. On your day of departure, most hotels ask you to vacate your room by noon. If you fail to do so, the hotel has the right to charge you for an extra night. If you discuss it with reception in advance, most hotels will agree a late check-out time.

RESTAURANTS

With seventy different kinds of cuisine on offer in the capital, you can eat as well, or better in London as you can in Paris, Rome, New York or LA. There's been a revolution in British cooking, and it's hard to find soggy vegetables and over-cooked meat, even if you want to! The brigade of ambitious British chefs are inventive and iconoclastic, and their cooking shows off the glory of British ingredients.

London's Indian restaurants range from the cheap and filling to the expensive and impressive. Brick Lane, just east of the City, is lined with curry and balti houses, while there are more elegant establishments dotted all round town. Don't be scared that the food might be too hot and spicy – dishes can be adapted to inexperienced palates and stomachs. If in doubt, ask for advice. The Chinese community in China Town, just north of Leicester Square, is teeming with restaurants, and you can buy a multitude of Chinese ingredients from the supermarkets if you fancy doing some Chinese cooking at home. Vying for your

interest are British, Italian (not just pasta and pizza), Thai, French, Turkish, Greek, North American (and not just hamburgers), Vietnamese and Sri Lankan restaurants.

Eating out isn't a formal event, so dress code is usually casual, unless you're going to a smarter restaurant where you have to book way ahead.

Service, usually 12.5%, isn't included in the price, and the policy of the restaurant will usually be printed on the menu. If it isn't clear, ask when you order. Sometimes a discretionary service charge is added to your bill. If you're not satisfied with the service you're not obliged to pay it. Also, watch out for credit card slips that are left blank in the hope that you'll add an amount for service when in fact this is already included in the bill. Don't tip in pubs.

Not all restaurants have a non-smoking area – it's not obligatory in the UK. It's best to check by phone in advance if you want to avoid other people's smoke.

Nowadays you can get something to eat at all hours

of the day and night in London, but restaurants usually have set times for lunch or dinner service and usually close one day a week.

TEA V COFFEE

You can still get a good cup of tea, accompanied by scones, crumpets or cucumber sandwiches. The Fountain in Fortnum & Masons on Piccadilly will come up trumps or, if you want a full, traditional tea, go to a grand hotel where they do it in true English style – silver service, sandwiches with crusts removed and cakes on a stand.

But London is bobbing on a sea of cappuccino froth. Italian sandwich bars used to be good for a strong cup of espresso. Now every street corner has a smart new coffee house where you can order from a dazzling range – short, strong and black, tall, skinny, frothy, caf, de-caf, with syrup, with chocolate or with cinnamon. The choice is enough to make your head spin. But the coffee is good and it's a new way of life.

HOTELS

Bond Street

Claridge's★★★★

Brook St., W1
⊖ **Bond Street**
☎ **020 7629 8860**
🖷 **020 7499 2210**
www.claridges.co.uk

Claridge's is an Art-Deco palace of great style. The line of limousines outside and the to-ing and fro-ing of ladies who lunch, 'A' list royals and international jet-setters are indicative of just how smart it is. Service is perfection and it has that quiet self-assurance that goes with international luxury.

Marylebone

La Place★★

17 Nottingham Pl., W1
⊖ **Baker Street**
☎ **020 7486 2323**
🖷 **020 7486 4335**

'La Place' isn't very expensive (under £110–130) for the district. It's close to the Oxford Street department stores and the waxworks of Madame Tussaud's. The hotel's restaurant has been done up and offers a menu of grills and Swiss cuisine, an unusual combination that sounds too intriguing to miss.

The Landmark Hotel★★★

222 Marylebone Rd, NW1
⊖ **Marylebone**
☎ **020 7631 8000**
🖷 **020 7631 8033**

A gigantic atrium, eight storeys high, links the rooms in this building that was once the headquarters of the British Railways Board. When it was converted, the rooms weren't made smaller, so they remain huge. The facilities are excellent, with a swimming pool, sauna, Turkish bath and gym, available to the hotel's guests at any time of day or night.

HAZLITT'S
1718

Soho

Hazlitt's★★★

6 Frith St., W1
⊖ **Tottenham Court Road**
☎ **020 7434 1771**
🖷 **020 7439 1524**

This establishment occupies three 18th-century houses in the heart of Soho. Its panelled walls are covered in small paintings and it's a favourite with the artistic fraternity. A nice touch is provided by the neo-Classical baths with feet in the shape of lion's paws.

Piccadilly

22 Jermyn Street★★★

22 Jermyn St., SW1
⊖ **Piccadilly Circus**
☎ **020 7734 2353**
🖷 **020 7734 0750**

Fresh flowers in every room, a far better supply of writing

materials than the usual dull postcards and thin paper and one of the best hotel gyms in London. As well as all this, it's in a glamourous, stylish street, famous for gentleman's outfitters', made-to-measure shirts and shoes, toiletries and one of the few traditional barber's left in the city.

South Kensington

Five Sumner Place★★

5 Sumner Pl., SW7
⊖ **South Kensington**
☎ **020 7584 7586**
🖷 **020 7823 9962**

This hotel won the prize for the best small hotel in London in 1991 and 1993, awarded by the Tourist Office. It occupies a beautiful Victorian house, and breakfast is served in a conservatory looking onto a very pretty garden.

Swiss House Hotel★★

171 Old Brompton Rd, SW5
⊖ **Gloucester Road**
☎ **020 7373 2769**
🖷 **020 7373 4983**

This isn't your usual bed and breakfast establishment. The entrance has lovely climbing plants at the front door and you're given a warm, friendly welcome by the staff. The rooms have high ceilings and are amazingly clean and spacious. However, you'll be charged a 5%

☎ 020 7730 1048
🖶 020 7730 2574

If you love flowers, this Georgian hotel is the place for you. Its interior is decorated in Laura Ashley designs, the rooms are smart and spotless, and the four-poster beds are just the thing for a romantic weekend.

The Willet ★★★

32 Sloane Gardens, SW1
⊖ **Sloane Square**
☎ 020 7824 8415
🖶 020 7730 4830

You'll love this discreetly luxurious red-brick hotel situated among the grand Victorian residences near Sloane Square. It has everything to ensure your comfort and the English breakfast is excellent.

The Claverley ★★★

13-14 Beaufort Gardens, SW3
⊖ **Knightsbridge**
☎ 020 7589 8541
🖶 020 7584 3410

This hotel is most conveniently situated for dropping off the purchases you've made at Harrods, particularly if you want to stay somewhere where the style suits the locality. From bathrooms, to breakfast, to service, everything is fit for a queen. Coffee, tea and newspapers are provided free of charge.

Number Eleven ★★★★

11, Cadogan Gardens, SW3
⊖ **Sloane Square**
☎ 020 7730 34 26
🖶 020 7730 52 17

This is one of the best-kept secrets in London. From the outside there's nothing to suggest there's a hotel here at all. This was one of the first hotels to be established in a private house, and a great many celebrities come and stay here incognito.

supplement if you pay your bill by credit card.

Sloane Square/ Knightsbridge

The Sloane Hotel ★★★

29 Draycott Pl., SW3
⊖ **Sloane Square**
☎ 020 7581 5757
🖶 020 7584 1348

This little hotel is furnished with antiques. What's more, if you see a piece you like, you can it buy it and take it home. The owners are passionate collectors, who sell off their furniture bit by bit so they can buy more.

Basil Street Hotel ★★★

8 Basil St., SW3
⊖ **Knightsbridge**
☎ 020 7581 3311
🖶 020 7581 3693

This hotel is home to the Parrot Club, one of London's women's clubs, so it's mainly patronised by women. But men and women alike can admire its beautiful furniture and lovely little lounges. You'll find it just behind Harrod's.

Woodville House ★★

107 Ebury St., SW1
⊖ **Sloane Square**

The lounge has a fireplace and looks out onto a lovely winter garden. The overall atmosphere is that of a luxurious town house that's elegantly decorated and furnished. They can organise the hire of a Rolls Royce with chauffeur for a day.

Bloomsbury

Ruskin Hotel★

23-4 Montague St., WC1
⊖ **Russell Square or Holborn**
☎ **020 7636 7388**
🅕 **020 7323 1662.**

The best thing about this hotel is its location. All the rooms have a view over the east wing of the British Museum. English breakfast is included in the very modest room prices, but you won't find a telephone in your room They'll pin up any messages for you on a board near the lobby. The hotel is very well run and has been under the same ownership for 17 years.

Russell Hotel★★★

Russell Sq., WC1
⊖ **Russell Square**
☎ **020 7837 6470**
🅕 **020 7837 2857**

It's best to ask for a room overlooking the garden of this enormous Victorian hotel. The interior design and atmosphere are staid and very respectable

Academy Hotel★★★

17-21 Gower St., WC1
⊖ **Goodge Street**
☎ **020 7631 4115**
🅕 **020 7636 3442**

This hotel, which occupies three Georgian residences just near University College, London, doesn't have the soulless interior that its reasonable prices

might lead you to expect. It also has a very pleasant garden and the food served in the restaurant is delicious.

Blooms Hotel★★★

7 Montague St., WC1
⊖ **Russell Square**
☎ **020 7323 1717**
🅕 **020 7636 6498**

Located in the literary district of Bloomsbury, Blooms Hotel prides itself on regularly adding new

books to its library, all of which can borrowed by guests. It has only 27 rooms and the garden overlooking the British Museum nearby complements the pleasant, relaxing atmosphere of this establishment. Prices are, however, rather high (£150 for a double).

Hampstead

La Gaffe★★

107-11 Heath St., NW3
⊖ **Hampstead**
☎ **020 7435 4941**
🅕 **020 7794 7592**

Though not in central London, this hotel is ideally situated in the heart of Hampstead and it isn't too expensive. The rooms aren't large, but they're very pretty and you can also sample the cuisine of the Italian restaurant run by the owners. NB all rooms are non-smoking.

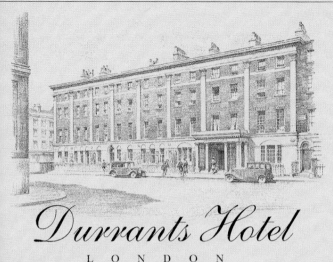

Durrants Hotel
L O N D O N

Oxford Street

Edward Lear Hotel★★

28-30 Seymour St., W1
⊖ **Marble Arch**
☎ **020 7402 5401**
📠 **020 7706 3766**

This Georgian house has been fully restored. It's situated just near Oxford Street and used to be the home of Edward Lear, the 19th-century English humourist. Today the hotel has two charming lounges and a breakfast room (no other meals are served). The rooms at the back are quieter. Good value for money.

Durrants Hotel★★★

George St., W1
⊖ **Bond Street**
☎ **020 7935 8131**
📠 **020 7487 3510**

This hotel used to be a post house and is situated in an ideal location between Oxford Street and Regent's Park. The atmosphere is one of comfort – all leather and wood with a 'batchelor' feel – and the service is punctillious. It's a pity the rooms are rather small.

Covent Garden

Fielding Hotel★★

4 Broad Court, Bow St., WC2
⊖ **Covent Garden**
☎ **020 7836 8305**
📠 **020 7497 0064**

This is one of the few interesting hotels in the theatre district. It's in a quiet pedestrian street lit by 19th-century gaslights, and was named after Henry Fielding, who carried out his duties at the Bow Street Magistrates Court round the corner, opposite the Royal Opera House. The interior is filled with plants and flowers and the rooms are individual and unusual – none of the walls seem to be built at right-angles. It isn't too expensive (about £80 for a double room).

THE FIELDING HOTEL

RESTAURANTS

Covent Garden and Strand

Rules★★
(Traditional English)

35 Maiden Lane, WC2
⊖ Covent Garden
☎ 020 7836 5314

Rules, founded in 1798, is the oldest restaurant in London. It specialises in classic game dishes but the cooking has nothing old-fashioned about it. The waiters are garbed in traditional attire but patrons can be less formal. From 12 August, the opening of the grouse season, Rules produces exceptional game dishes. It's open noon-11.15pm in the week, or 10.45pm on Sundays.

Simpson's in the Strand★★★
(Traditional English)

100 Strand, WC2
⊖ Charing Cross
☎ 020 7836 9112

This restaurant has been catering for Londoners since 1828 and will serve you excellent roast beef in a traditional club interior. But this is the place to come for a sumptuous breakfast of salmon and lamb's liver, to mention only two of the lighter dishes. The service is impressive, with silverware passing back and forth. It's a very smart place where you're expected to dress. Men are strongly advised to wear a jacket and tie.

Green Park

Greenhouse★★★
(Traditional English)

27A Hay's Mews, W1
⊖ Green Park
☎ 020 7499 3331

This restaurant occupies the ground floor of an amazing building dating from the inter-war years. The interior is airy and light and the atmosphere, like the service, is young and alert. Gary Rhodes, a celebrity TV chef, has resuscitated English cuisine and you must try the smoked haddock with Welsh rarebit or the delicious lemon meringue pie. It's not cheap, but because it's very popular you're advised to book well in advance.

Coast★★★
(Modern English)

26B Albemarle St., W1
⊖ Green Park
☎ 020 7495 5999

Back in the mid-90s, Coast's cool, cutting-edge interior and original cuisine marked it out for gastro stardom. It was flooded with accolades. Come 2000, and a new culinary tide, Coast is marooned as a slightly outmoded island of 90's taste. The food is a costly plateful and the wine's expensive.

Holborn

St John★★
(Traditional English)

26 St John St., EC1
⊖ Farringdon (Holborn)
☎ 020 7251 0848

This restaurant offers very good English cooking at realistic prices. Don't expect an extraordinary decor, but the service is more than decent. Try the salted pork liver and make sure you try one of the puddings, which are among some of the best in town.

Cheaper meals are on offer in the basement at lunchtime, which could give you the opportunity for a pleasant break in a day's shopping in this busy part of town.

Criterion Brasserie★★★
(Modern French)
Piccadilly Circus
⊖ Leiscester Square
☎ 020 7930 0488

The Criterion has a magnificent, glittering, neo-Byzantine interior. It's owned by Marco Pierre White, the 'enfant terrible' of British cooking, who wanted to bring fine cuisine to all. The dishes are inventive, the prices aren't crazy, and the *Cappuccino* (chicken soup) is simply divine.

Piccadilly Circus

The Square★★★
(Modern English)
6-10 Bruton St.
⊖ Green Park
☎ 020 7839 8787

The interior design is minimalist and very 1960's. The cooking was by English chef Gary Rhodes and, with other restaurants, it made it acceptable to eat until 11.30pm in the very centre of London. The grilled wild salmon, served with risotto, hits the spot and the desserts are very good.

New Mayflower★★
(Chinese)
68-70 Shaftesbury Av., W1
⊖ Piccadilly Circus
☎ 020 7734 9207

This restaurant consists of a labyrinth of little rooms where you can sample very fine Cantonese cuisine. Don't be afraid to try some of the bolder combinations, such as chicken liver with seafood (squid, octopus, scallops and shrimps), which are a real discovery and truly delicious. It's best to go in the evening as you can eat until very late at night and it's always busy.

Mitsukoshi★★★
(Japanese)
Dorland House,
14-20 Lower Regent St., SW1
⊖ Piccadilly Circus
☎ 020 7930 0317

You might have a bit of trouble deciphering the menu, which is transcribed, but in the main not translated, but you can't go wrong if you stick to the sashimi, which is some of the best and most varied in town. You won't be disappointed by the grills either. There's also a wide range of places to sit, from tatami mats to a bar or classic European tables. Enough to satisfy the connoisseur.

Soho

Alastair Little★★
(Modern Italian)
49 Frith St., W1
⊖ Leicester Square
☎ 020 7734 5183

Alastair Little is a serious chef who produces highly innovative cuisine using fresh ingredients.

Wheelers★★
(Fish)
19 Old Compton St., W1
⊖ Leicester Square
☎ 020 7437 2706

Wheelers is a restaurant chain with branches all over London. They serve some of the best fresh fish cooked in traditional styles, either plain or with lots of sauce. It's of very high quality, if a little expensive.

Ikkyu★
(Japanese)

7-9 Newport Pl., WC1
⊖ Leicester Square
☎ 020 7439 3554

This Japanese restaurant is spread over two floors. Go downstairs and, if possible, occupy one of the two alcoves, where you can take off your shoes and eat sitting on tatami mats round a low communal table. If you're a newcomer to Japanese cuisine, try a *bento*, which offers you a range of different specialities, or order a *yakitori* if you're not keen on raw fish (*sushi* and *sashimi*).

Chelsea

Bibendum Oyster Bar★★★
(Fish)

Michelin House,
81 Fulham Rd, SW3
⊖ South Kensington
☎ 020 7589 1480

You can't miss this restaurant, which is situated off the entrance hall of the magnificent Michelin building. As they don't take reservations, you have to queue for a table and it's better to wait a few more minutes to get one in the dining room rather than outside in the main hall. The best thing to order here

is the seafood platter, which you can then follow up with one of the very fine desserts.

Chutney Mary★★★
(Indian)

535 King's Rd, SW10
☎ 020 7351 3113

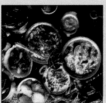

Don't be intimidated by the long menu, because this restaurant offers an excellent choice of the finest cuisine from northern India and dishes combining Indian and Western influences. If you can't make up your mind, you can always order a sampler of a range of different dishes

which, unusually for this type of presentation, won't leave you hungry. Otherwise, try ordering lamb with dried apricots or pick something at random. You won't be disappointed.

Salloos★★★
(Pakistani)

62-64 Kinnerton St., SW1
⊖ Knightsbridge
☎ 020 7235 4444

This is a specifially Pakistani restaurant, serving some of the best meat dishes you could imagine – the tandoori dishes are particularly good. It also has a very good wine list, which is unusual for this type of restaurant.

Hampstead

Cucina★★
(Italian)

45A South End Rd, NW3
⊖ Belsize Park
☎ 020 7435 7814

This restaurant only opened in 1994, but it has established a reputation for both the cuisine on offer and its customer care. Several good fish dishes are served, with more exotic ingredients, such as mango, in a very simple, unfussy decor.

Oxford Street

Nico Central ★★★
(French)

35 Great Portland St., W1
⊖ Oxford Circus
☎ 020 7436 8846

Cheaper and more accessible than its big brother, Nico at Ninety, this is the poshest of French restaurants. Nico Central is very attractive and its cuisine is influenced by Provençal cooking. Dishes are wonderfully tasty.

Wagamama
(Japanese/noodles)

4 Streatham St., at the corner of Coptic St. WC1
⊖ Tottenham Court Road
☎ 020 7323 9223

This is a very popular noodle bar. There are often queues, but don't let that put you off because they move very quickly. The various soups with noodles (£5-£7), with meat, fish or just vegetables, are excellent. The entire restaurant is non-smoking.

Fitzrovia

Chez Gérard ★★
(French)

8 Charlotte St., W1
⊖ Goodge Street
☎ 020 7636 4975

If nothing but steak (and good steak at that) and chips will do, then make your way here. As you might imagine from the name, the atmosphere is French. The service can be somewhat casual, but all the French classics are offered here; starters include snails in garlic butter and the steaks come in French cuts; entrecôte, fillet, Château-

briand, côte de boeuf and 'bavette'. Fish dishes are simply grilled and puddings are classic – crème brûlée and Tarte Tatin.

North Sea Fish Restaurant ★
(Fish and chips)

7-8 Leigh St., WC1
⊖ Russell Square
☎ 020 7387 5892

This restaurant offers all kinds of fish to eat in or take away, doused with salt and vinegar and wrapped in paper. But if you want eat in a fish and chip restaurant without actually eating fish and chips, you can always try the home-made vegetable soup instead.

Islington

Upper Street Fish Shop ★

324 Upper St., N1
⊖ Angel
☎ 020 7359 1401

You'll be surprised to find this very popular fish and chip restaurant in a sort of French-style bistrot. There's a good choice on the menu, including undoubtedly the best fish soup in town, and you'll get generous portions at a very reasonable price.

shopping Practicalities

SHOP OPENING TIMES

Shopping in London is fast is becoming a 24-hours-a-day, 7-days-a-week activity. Food shops are usually open 9am-6pm, Mondays to Saturdays, though a good number close at 8pm and some open on Sundays. Shops selling clothes or household goods usually open at 10am. Closing time is often 6pm, but many stores have a late-night until 7pm, or sometimes 9pm, one evening a week Shops don't close for lunch. More and more shops also open on Sundays, though some of the large department stores are closed all day. To be sure of finding that special item you wanted to buy, it's a good idea to look for it on Saturday; so you can spend Sunday wandering around at your leisure and going into any of the 'cool' clothes shops that take your fancy. Most junk markets are open on Sundays starting quite early in the morning and usually packing up around 1pm, but Portobello market is open on Fridays and Saturdays. On Sunday afternoon you could make a trip to Hampstead, where two busy streets stay open for business until the evening.

HOW TO PAY

Most shops and large stores accept international credit cards (American Express, Mastercard, Diner's Club,

and Visa). Some, such as John Lewis, have their own store card but usually also take debit or credit cards swiped through a machine.
There are some pickpockets in London, as in any other major city, so be sure to keep a close watch on your money and cards. If you do lose a card, or have the misfortune to have yours stolen, you should call the appropriate number immediately and report it.

Visa
☎ 0800 895 082
American Express
☎ 01273 696 933
Diner's Club
☎ 0800 460 800
Mastercard
☎ 01702 351 303

If you're in London from overseas, sterling traveller's cheques are accepted in many places. If you have them in any other currency you'll find that you're penalised by the exchange rate.

DUTY FREE

If you travel to London by plane, you can take advantage of the duty-free shopping facilities, which aren't available in Eurostar stations. However the European Union's new internal regulations have abolished duty free between European Union countries. If you leave London from an intercontinental air terminal, you'll still find duty free shopping at Heathrow.

Heathrow has a very impressive Swatch shop with some truly unbeatable prices. You can also get cameras and hi-fi equipment at knock-down prices. There's also a small branch of Harrods here. In the self-service section you should forget the cigarettes and go for the chocolates and alcoholic drinks. The prices may not seem that much cheaper than at home but the bottles all contain 1 litre/2.2 pints rather than the more usual 75 cl.

Prices are always marked in the UK, even in shop windows. Don't even think about haggling in a shop, but it's a different story in the markets, and part of the fun of browsing the market stalls is trying to make a deal and getting the price down by a few pounds.

FREIGHT AND DELIVERY

If you buy a piece of furniture or some other bulky item, you can always have it sent home. You should give the delivery company a photocopy of your receipt and they will make out a delivery slip.

All the large stores offer this service, but you can also use a private shipping company. Here are some useful addresses:

Radford International
A1 Radford Business Centre, Radford Way, Billericay, Essex
☎ **020 8208 1677 or 020 8554 8333 (Mon.-Fri. 8am-6pm, Sat. 9am-1pm).**

This company will transport parcels and packages of any size and will give you a free estimate.

The Packing Shop
Unit KNL London Stone Business Estate, Broughton St., SW8
☎ **020 7498 3255 (Mon.-Fri. 9am-6pm).**

The Packing Shop specialises in packing and carrying fragile items. Its express service guarantees you delivery within one week.

Lockson Service Ltd
29 Broomfield St., London E14.
☎ **020 7515 8600 (Mon.–Sat. 9am–5pm)**

This company does a lot of work for the stallholders of the Portobello Road market. They carry all kinds of objects, including that Royal Doulton teapot you've just acquired and are terrified of breaking. Better still, they're open on Saturdays.

CUSTOMS

If you're a citizen of a country in the European Union, you don't have to pay customs duty on antiques, works of art or more ordinary items. At customs all you need do is present your receipt showing the name and address of the supplier, the price paid including and excluding tax, a description of the article and your own name and address. This documentation will be sufficient, no matter how much the items you're taking home are worth. You won't have to make any special declaration. If, however, you're importing counterfeit or stolen items, you may be charged with receiving or possessing illegal or stolen goods.

If you're from North America, Australia or New Zealand, check with your own customs service about what you're entitled to take home. Its best to avoid nasty surprises when you get back after your trip.

Buy only from reputable suppliers and be wary of anything that looks like a bargain. If you buy a work of art, you can ask for a certificate of authenticity, which the supplier is obliged to provide you with. You absolutely *must* keep all receipts. You may be asked to show them at customs and they'll be useful if you want to sell one of the items you've bought at a later date or if you're ever the victim of a robbery and need the information to fill in the claim form for insurance purposes.

FINDING YOUR WAY AROUND

Next to each address in the Shopping and Nightlife chapters you'll find a reference given in brackets for the map on pp. 78-79 .

TRUE CLASSICS

The shops listed here are *la crème de la crème*, the quintessence of what shopping in London has to offer. They're indispensable ports of call if you want to know what British style is all about. Classic shops can be expensive, but, as their designs never go out of style and can come with a lifetime's guarantee, they're an investment – even down to your favourite pair of Doc Martens'.

designer label offering the brand's traditional quality in younger styles, trench coats re-cut in silk and a range of red, brown and beige sportswear-influenced separates, with velcro fastenings. Even the distinctive house check has been reinvented.

Swaine Adeney Briggs

10 Old Bond St., W1 (B2)
☎ **020 7409 7277**
✪ **Bond Street**
Mon.-Sat. 10am-6pm.

A smart, slightly formal 'hunting lodge' atmosphere with hunting trophies, wood panelling and riding tackle hanging on the wall (saddles £800-£1500).

Thomas Burberry

191 Regent St., SW1 (B2)
☎ **020 7734 4060**
✪ **Piccadilly Circus**
Mon.-Wed. 10am-6pm,
Thu.-Fri. 10am-7pm,
Sat. 9.30am-6.30pm
Sun noon-6pm.

The classic cuts of Burberry's main collection are stylish and pricey, but the look has had a makeover and been re-launched as a

Aquascutum

100 Regent St., SW1 (B2)
☎ **020 7734 6090**
✪ **Piccadilly Circus**
Mon.-Sat. 10am-6.30pm,
Thu. 10am-7.30pm.

Aquascutum is still a British institution, though it fell into Japanese hands in 1990. The clothes are well made and unsurprising, the atmosphere more stockbroker than punk, with classically-cut men's shirts and cashmere jumpers. Ask for the catalogue – it isn't terrifically useful, but it's lovely to look at.

Stephen Jones

36 Great Queen St., WC2 (C2)
☎ 020 7242 0770
⊖ Covent Garden
Tue.-Fri. 10am-6pm,
Thu. 10am-7pm.
Sat. by appointment.

Stephen Jones is regarded as one of the finest milliners in Europe. He designs highly original and discreetly elegant hats, that can be worn with confidence and without ostentation. For what they are, the prices aren't outrageous, and if you have a special occasion that demands a special creation, this is the place to come.

London House

51 Great Russell St., WC1 (C2)
☎ 020 7430 2547
⊖ Tottenham Court Road
Mon.-Sat. 9am-6pm,
Sun. 11.30am-6.30pm.

This shop, right opposite the British Museum, is aimed mostly at tourists and sells woollens, scarves, tartans, kilts, Harris Tweed and children's things. It isn't very expensive and also has a bureau de change. Handy for Sunday shopping.

Herbert Johnson

30 New Bond St., W1 (B2)
☎ 020 7408 1174
⊖ Bond Street
Mon.-Sat. 10am-6pm.

This traditional hatters, which creates styles for men and women,

has an in-house team of milliners and about a hundred different types of hat on sale, ranging from the classic to the highly unusual. This is the place to get a man's cap of the 'typically English' variety.

House of Cashmere

10-11 Burlington Arcade, W1 (B2)
☎ 020 7499 1349
⊖ Piccadilly Circus
Mon.-Fri. 9am-5.30pm
Sat. 9.30am-5.30pm.

Very good quality classic styles in cashmere and cashmere only. Outrageously high prices and perfunctory courtesy from the sales staff who are used to dealing with clients who have several Swiss bank accounts.

Berk

6, 20-21 and 46-49 Burlington Arcade, W1 (B2)
☎ 020 7493 0028
⊖ Piccadilly Circus
Mon.-Sat. 9am-5.30pm.

These shops seem to occupy half the Burlington Arcade. One of

them, at nos 20-21, also sells clothing from Mulberry (well known for their leather goods) and Burberry, which can come in handy if you want to make sure the different elements of your outfit go together without having to walk miles. Loads of choice.

Tops

217 Regent St., W1 (B2)
☎ 020 7437 2419
⊖ Oxford Circus
Mon.-Sat. 9.30am-6.30pm.

There are 5000 different fabrics on sale here by the metre, including the inevitable wool and cashmere (from £15 to £1000 a metre), as well as Harris Tweed. Don't panic, the sales staff will help you with your calculations to make sure you buy the right amount.

> ### MEASURING HOW MUCH FABRIC YOU NEED
>
> If you're planning to buy a Liberty print by the metre to make a tablecloth, measure the length and width of your table before you leave for London and add to each the overhang you want. For napkins, measure some you already have and allow 1 inch/2.5cm for the hems. When it comes to suits, all the shops will offer to do the calculations for you, so you don't have to worry.

MacKenzie's

169 Piccadilly, W1 (B2)
☎ 020 7495 5514
⊖ Piccadilly Circus
Mon.-Fri. 10am-6.30pm,
Wed. 10am-7pm, Sat. 10am-
6pm, Sun. 11am-5.30pm.

Woollens and tartans, classic
styles and fair prices, with scarves
from £10 to £48 and V-necked
cashmere jumpers from £45.

Joseph

77 Fulham Rd, SW3 (A3)
☎ 020 7823 9500
⊖ Sloane Square
Mon.-Fri. 10am-6.30pm,
Wed. 10am-7pm, Sat.
10am-6pm, Sun. noon-5pm.

Joseph's designs are known and
sold worldwide; but this is the
original store. It's very large and
well laid out with perfectly-cut
trousers and knitwear in modern,
fluid styles and unusual yarns.
The place is often packed.

Browns

18, 23-27, 38, 50 and 62
South Molton St., W1 (B2)
⊖ Bond Street
☎ 020 7491 7833
Mon.-Sat. 10am-6pm,
Thu. 10am-7pm.

All the big name designers are
available in this group of shops
that run the length of the street.
Also discounted designer clothes
(see p. 59).

Doctor Martens' Department Store

1-4 King St., WC2 (C2)
☎ 020 7497 1460
⊖ Covent Garden
Mon.-Sat. 9.30am-7pm, Sun.
noon-6pm, Thu. 9.30am-8pm.

Six floors devoted not just to the
cult footwear but also to a line of
skater-style street styles worn
by young people who
aren't quite as sporty as
their outfits would
suggest. There's also
a hairdresser's and
a café. Doc
Martens have
become a basic
item of clothing
and customers range
from young, trendy
types to the more sedate.
The Doc Marten classic
black eight-holed boot
costs about £55, and they're
so comfortable you'll soon wonder
how you ever coped without them.

Paul Smith

40-44 Floral St., WC2 (C2)
☎ 020 7379 7133
⊖ Covent Garden
Westbourne House
122 Kensington Park Rd,
W11 (off map)
☎ 020 7727 3553
⊖ Notting Hill Gate

Mon.-Sat. 10.30am-6.30pm,
Thu. 10.30am-7pm.

The cult designer of British men's
fashions recently opened a
women's department. Everything
here is very smart and elegant
without ever being conventional,
and is presented on shelves of dark
wood. In Langley Court, turn right
on your way out for Paul Smith
Jeans, the 'b' line, or, if you turn
left instead, Paul Smith Kids,
where, among the wares on offer,
you can buy fun children's hats in
the shape of various animals.

The Mulberry House

11/12 Gees Court, St
Christopher's Pl., W1 (B2)
☎ 020 7493 2546
⊖ Bond Street
Mon.-Sat. 10am-6pm,
Thu. 10am-7pm.

Smart, elegant leather clothes and
accessories, all in good taste and
drawing mainly on hunting styles.

Prices are high and the quality can be disappointing (yokes in fake leather when you'd expect to find the real thing).

N Peal

71 Burlington Arcade, W1 (B2)
☎ 020 7493 0912
⊖ Piccadilly Circus
Every day 9.30am-6pm.

The cult shop for cashmere connoisseurs. These are without a doubt the finest in London,

but you'll pay at least £200 for a jumper. Exceptional quality and an enormous range of colours make this shop a priority if you love jumpers or cashmere.

Church's

133 New Bond St., W1 (B2)
☎ 020 7493 1474
⊖ Bond Street
Mon.-Sat. 9am-6.30pm,
Thu. 9am-7pm.

Church's shoes have fans in many countries. Some people keep theirs for more than 20 years, real

THE SALES

The January Sales are still a tradition, and the summer ones are still held in June. Some shops start clearance sales even before Christmas so you can hunt down a bargain present, and since the winter collections are sold off, there's still a lot of the season left for you to flaunt your purchase. But even if it's usually warm back home, the electric atmosphere in London's big stores during this period must be seen to be believed. The hysteria in Harrods and Harvey Nichols is a real experience. Some shops are now luring customers with huge reductions of up to 50 or 60% off the original prices, so if you time it right you can get a real bargain. But, be warned, it can be absolute madness. Outside the sales periods, lots of shops run promotions, so look out for the sale rails.

obsessives have several pairs in the same style. Women can also indulge as Church's have a range of classic, well-cut women's shoes on sale here. There's less choice but the colours are more wide-ranging with reds and blues among the classic tans and blacks. (see p. 57). The briefcases are to be treasured for a lifetime.

Westaway and Westaway

65 Great Russell St.,
WC1 (C2)
☎ 020 7405 4479.
⊖ Tottenham Court Road
Mon.-Sat. 9am-5.30pm,
Sun. 10.30am-5.30pm.

Two shops side by side. One is for men and women, the other for children. Both sell good quality woollens at very affordable prices (see p. 53).

WOMEN'S FASHION

London Fashion Week has become a trend-setting fixture in the catwalk calendar. Everyone shows here, from classic designers who dress 'A' list celebs to up-and-at-it streetwear for a unique, outrageous look for an evening or the whole season. But start with beauty that's skin deep: pampering, perfumed potions and luxurious lingerie.

PAMPER YOURSELF

Jo Malone

150 Sloane St., SW3 (B3)
☎ **020 7720 0202**
⊖ Sloane Square
Mon.-Sat. 9.30am-6.30pm,
Wed. 9.30am-7pm.

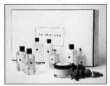

Scent your bath with exotic oils or anoint your skin with fragrant creams perfumed with smouldering spices or light spring flowers. Jo Malone's sleek, chic, cream and black emporium has a selection of original perfumes, bath oils and shower gels, and sumptuous skin-care preparations.

DESIGNER WEAR

Rigby & Peller

2 Hans Rd, SW3 (A3)
☎ **020 7589 9293**
⊖ Knightsbridge
Mon.-Sat. 9.30am-6.30pm,
Wed. 9.30am-7pm.

Any woman's dream. Underwear to give you the body you've always dreamed of. Bras from £50, made-to-measure from £250. Refreshingly informal and friendly. There's also an elegant

selection of ready-made lingerie and nightwear from La Perla, Gottex and Prima Donna. It's round the corner from Harrods.

Caroline Charles

56-57 Beauchamp Pl.,
SW3 (A3)
☎ **020 7589 5850**
⊖ Knightsbridge
Mon.-Sat. 10am-6pm.

This very aristocratic shop looks like the drawing-room of a private house, with mantlepieces and mirrors. Caroline Charles is, after all, dressmaker to princesses, and time is no object here, any more than money (at least £200 for an impeccably cut skirt). You'll be in excellent hands and will get the best advice, but your partner may find the time passes rather slowly.

East

192 Fulham Rd, SW10 (A3)
☎ **020 7351 5070**
⊖ South Kensington
Mon.-Sat. 10am-6pm,
Sun. noon-5pm.

This shop sells unusual, handmade clothes with influences from India and Japan, a reminder that Great Britain was once the centre of a global empire. Between £50 and £100 for a dress.

Episode

53 Brompton Road, SW3 (B2)
☎ 020 7589 5724
⊖ Knightsbridge
Mon.-Sat. 10am-6pm,
Thu. 10am-7pm.

Smart, sharp designs for day and evening. Episode uses unusual cloth and elegantly-patterned silk weaves that are intriguingly cut for a stylish look. Their ranges of co-ordinating tops and soft knitwear are a steal.

Whistles

12-14 St Christopher's Pl.,
W1 (B2)
☎ 020 7487 4484
⊖ Bond Street
Mon.-Sat. 10am-6pm,
Thu. 10am-7pm.

In the dozen-or-so years that this shop has been around, it has continually discovered new designers, selling their clothes at normal ready-to-wear prices. You can find branches throughout London (items from £20 to £1,500).

Malapa

41 Clerkenwell Rd, EC1 (C1)
☎ 020 7499 8368
⊖ Farringdon
Mon.-Fri. 10.30am-7pm,
Thu. 10.30am-7.30pm,
Sat. noon-5pm.

Step inside to explore designs from the latest idols of the fashion world. You can also be first to admire the beautiful new styles from the great British designers of tomorrow. There's something here to suit every taste and – even more importantly – every pocket.

Formes

313 Brompton Rd, SW3 (A3)
☎ 020 7584 3337
⊖ South Kensington
Mon.-Sat. 10am-6pm.

A shop for mothers-to-be that's a cut above the rest, since it sells designer clothes for pregant women (with belts that can be adjusted as your pregnancy develops).

Chic, ingenious clothes that will make you feel like expecting a baby more often.

Karen Millen

46 South Molton St., W1 (B2)
☎ 020 7495 5297
⊖ Bond Street
Mon.-Sat. 10am-6.30pm,
Thu. 10am-7.30pm.

This label has a number of outlets in London, and is one of the most interesting franchise names. The clothes are inexpensive and made from interesting fabrics and are as good looking as some well-known designer labels.

APC

40 Ledbury Rd, (off map)
☎ 020 7229 4933
⊖ Notting Hill Gate
Mon.-Sat. 10.30am-7pm.

All the APC designs for simple, unostentatious clothes.

CHECK YOUR SIZE

Visitors from outside the UK may find the sizes different from those they're used to, but the sales assistant should be able to help you find the perfect fit. See the conversion tables on p. 127 for more help.

STREET-SMART, HIP AND TRENDY

AdHoc/Boy

10-11 Moor St., W1 (C2)
☎ 020 7287 0911
⊖ Leicester Square
Mon.-Thu. 11am-7.30pm,
Fri.-Sat. 11am-8.30pm,
Sun. 1-6pm.

The best place to appreciate the more hysterical element in London fashions. As soon as you see the window-display, you'll be transfixed by the kitsch glitz. The clothes are completely wild (Lycra dresses with malibu trim and PVC catsuits), often provocative and not necessarily in the best possible taste. Treat yourself to a fun accessory – a wig, hair dye or nightmare nail varnish.

The Common Market

121 King's Rd, SW3 (A3)
☎ 020 7351 9361
⊖ Sloane Square
Mon.-Sun. 9.30am-7pm.

Don't be put off by the rather dull-sounding name or simple window display. Inside you'll find an enormous hall where creations by the trendiest designers of the day are presented. It's a real ready-to-wear supermarket, with G-Star jeans from £50 and little Diesel dresses.

Hype DF

48-52 Kensington High St., W8 (A2)
☎ 020 7937 3100
⊖ High St. Kensington
Mon.-Sat. 10am-6pm,
Thu. 10am-8pm,
Sun. noon-6pm

This shop remains faithful to the original principle of HyperHyper – which it has replaced – selling only young designers at affordable prices. Hunt out the stalls of Dexter

Wong, £15 for an almost transparent top, and Red or Dead gear. There's also a restaurant and a manicurist.

Bond International

10 Newburgh St, W1 (B2)
☎ 020 7437 0079
⊖ Oxford Circus
www.bondinternational.com
Mon.-Sat. 10.30am-6pm.

If you're longing for American hip-hop-style baggy pants, this shop will have you zinging with pleasure. T-shirts and jeans to suit. Stock includes Zoo York, Silas, Tender Loin, Haze and Addict and their own

Bond International label. Special edition shoes and trainers come from such makers as Stan Smith, Ramblers, Adidas, Wallabies and Desert Treks. They also stock stacks of graffiti images and books. It's the hiphoppiest.

Kensington Market

49-53 Kensington High St., W8 (A2)
☎ 020 7938 4343
⊖ High Street Kensington
Mon.-Sat. 9am-6pm,
Sun. noon-6pm.

A shadow of its former self but still wild and wacky. Rock-A-Cha sells retro clothing (zoot suits can be made to order), and there's a hyper-hip hairdresser (you wanted red dreads?), body-piercing and tattoos. Wendy's does great multi-coloured patent-leather studded belts, wrist-bands and dog-collars.

HANDBAGS

Bill Amberg

**10 Chepstow Rd, W11
(off map)
☎ 020 7727 3560
θ Notting Hill Gate
Mon.-Tue., Thu.-Sat. 10am-
6pm, Wed. 10am-7pm.**

Since the 1980s, Bill
Amberg has risen to the
top of the field in leather
accessories and his
collections are always
unusual. His most
recent creations are
particularly good,
especially the
sheepskin Puff Bag.
Some of the items
on show here
are way-out-
wild, others
simple, but all
are out-of-the-
ordinary, and no fashion-
conscious should consider
being seen without one.

SHOES

Manolo Blahnik

**49-51 Old Church St.,
Kings Rd, SW3 (A3)
☎ 020 7352 3863
θ Sloane Square
Mon.-Sat. 10am-6pm, Sat.
10.30am-5.30pm.**

Here refined ladies will find the
most elegant, irresistible styles

imaginable. The word 'resist' is
appropriate when the temptation
costs an average of £270, but it's
no crime to treat yourself.

Deliss

**15 St Albans Grove,
W8 (A3)
☎ 020 7938 2255
θ High Street
Kensington
Mon.-Fri. 9.30am-5.30pm,
Sat. noon-4pm.**

Have some exceptional shoes
made to measure, from
£390 a pair.

It won't mean waiting around in
London while they're made –
they'll be sent home to you as
soon as they're ready.

Patrick Cox

**8 Symons St., SW1 (A3)
☎ 020 7730 6504
θ Sloane Square
Mon.-Sat. 10am-6pm.**

The place to try if you want to buy
unusual British shoes. Modern
styles combined with superb
quality make these shoes a must
for any fashion-conscious woman
about town. Very
smart.

Red or Dead

**61 Neal St., WC2 (C2)
☎ 020 7379 7571
θ Covent Garden
Mon.-Fri. 10.30am-6.30pm,
Sat. 10am-6.30pm,
Sun. noon-5pm.**

You'll wear the shoes you
buy here for one season
only because they
follow fashion very
closely, but they
aren't very
expensive
(around £65,
some reduced
to £10 in the
sales).

SHOE SIZES

Women's shoe sizes may also be different in London from those at
home, but you'll find that the sales assistant will probably know
the international sizes, or check yourself on page 127. Don't forget
that while you're dashing around on your shopping spree your feet
may get hot and swollen, so make sure you consider the sizing
carefully before purchasing a pair of shoes.

MEN'S FASHION

There's nothing like a trip to London to enable you to bring a touch of class to your wardrobe. From Savile Row to Covent Garden, you'll find outfitters offering every style, from the latest fashions to classically tailored suits. However, you might have a problem finding a bowler hat!

James Lock & Co.

6 St James's St., SW1 (B2)
☎ 020 7930 8874
Ⓔ Green Park
Mon.-Fri. 9am-5.30pm,
Sat. 9.30am-5.30pm.

This hat shop, founded in the 18th century, is a London institution. It was here that the first bowler hats were sold, as they still are today. At James Lock, you'll also find all kinds of more wearable hats, like trilbies, and they stock some splendid panamas. You'll receive a very friendly reception, even if you want to educate yourself in headgear rather than buy something.

John Lobb

9 St James's St., SW1 (B2)
☎ 020 7930 3664
Ⓔ Green Park
Mon.-Fri. 9am-5.30pm,
Sat 9am-4.30pm.

As the quintessence of absolute luxury, here, for around £1,500, you can have an exceptional pair of shoes made to measure. You'll have to be a little bit patient, as making and delivery take rather a long time – it'll be about six months before you can slip your feet into the finest shoes in the world. The staff are very pleasant and there's a wonderful catalogue showing all the styles available with advice on how to maintain and care for your shoes (see p. 39).

Burro

19a Floral St., WC2 (C2)
☎ 020 7240 5120
Ⓔ Covent Garden
Mon.-Wed., Fri.-Sat.
10.30am-6.30pm,
Thu. 10.30am-7pm, Sun. 1-5pm.

Burro is a major menswear store and its collections make regular appearances on the Paris catwalks. The policy here is simple: no labels and sober, logo-free designs. From £100 for a pair of trousers.

TM Lewin & Sons

106 Jermyn St., SW1 (B2)
☎ 020 7930 4291
Ⓔ Piccadilly Circus
Mon.-Fri. 10am-6.30pm,
Thu. 10am-7pm,
Sat. 10am-6pm.

In this shop, you'll find a very impressive collection of shirts in

both classic and contemporary styles, made in all kinds of fabrics, and around 500 ties at very reasonable prices (£38 for a handmade tie). It's impossible not to find at least one to suit your taste.

Jones

15 Floral St., WC2 (C2)
☎ 020 7379 4299
Ⓔ Covent Garden
Mon.-Sat. 10am-6.30pm,
Sun. 1-5pm.

Floral Street is home to the greatest names in men's fashion, and Jones is a real mecca for all gentlemen. This shop has an exceptional range of designer clothes, including Christophe Lemaire, Dries Van Noten, Westwood and McQueen, to name but a few. From the presentation to the clothes themselves, everything here looks wonderful and is extremely tempting, so keep an eye on your wallet.

Gieves and Hawkes

1 Savile Row, W1 (B2)
☎ 020 7434 2001
⊖ Piccadilly Circus
Mon.-Tue. and Thu. 9am-7.30pm, Wed. 10am-7.30pm, Sat. 10am-6pm.
18 Lime St., EC3 (D2)
☎ 020 7283 4914
⊖ Monument
Mon.-Fri. 9am-6pm.

The most classic of all the classic tailors on Savile Row, *the* street for bespoke British tailoring. Given the clientele, the styles aren't exactly wild, but that's hardly what you come here for. The best cloth, expert cutting and tailoring, and an attention to detail that's a dying art. You can't put a price on perfection.

Austin Reed

103-113 Regent St., W1 (B2)
☎ 020 7734 6789
⊖ Piccadilly Circus
Mon.-Wed. Fri.-Sat. 10am-6.30pm., Thu. 10am-7.30pm, Sun. noon-5pm.

This large store, mostly for men's fashions, carries all the main international labels like Cerrutti and Hugo Boss, and it also has its own label. They offer every possible service, from a haircut to a shoe-shine, and tea and coffee are served free to customers.

Richard James

31 Savile Row, W1 (B2)
☎ 020 7434 0605
⊖ Piccadilly Circus
Mon.-Fri. 10am-6pm,
Sat. 11am-6pm.

Richard James is the least staid of all the Savile Row tailors, as he's more than willing to make

a suit in denim or a more unusual colour than black or grey (such as pistachio, for example). His imaginative approach is well-suited to men who want a style that's elegant without being too formal.

MADE TO MEASURE WAITING TIMES

H aving your shoes, shirts or suits made takes time. There's a six-month waiting-list at John Lobb, not including the time it takes to actually make up your order. Shirts take a few weeks (on average between 6 and 8), but you'll have to wait three to six months for a suit. Remember this if you're planning to wear Gieves & Hawkes at your wedding. On the other hand, there's nothing to stop you ordering even if you're only in London for the weekend, but it's a good idea to make an appointment by phone before you leave home.

Kent and Curven

39 St James's St., SW1 (B2)
☎ 020 7409 1955
⊖ Green Park
Mon.-Sat. 9.30am-6pm.

Opposite the Ritz, this shop has every jersey and cricket jumper imaginable. They're well laid out and presented on big wooden shelves. You don't need to

understand the subtleties of cricket to appreciate the jumpers that go with the game (£95).

Palomino

5 Flask Walk, NW3 (off map)
☎ 020 7431 9141
⊖ Hampstead Heath
Tue.-Sat. 10.30am-6pm,
Sun. noon-6pm.

Shirts and jumpers in relaxed styles at affordable prices, representative of 'Dress-down Friday Wear', the new business trend that allows men to leave their ties at home when they go to work on Fridays. Also gift ideas, such as fashion watches.

CHILDREN'S FASHION

It's now or never . . . Make your dreams come true and kit your little darlings out like heirs to the throne of England. While Marks & Spencer has good quality and modern design, you'll find a great many shops selling traditional dresses with Peter Pan collars and smocking.

Buckle My Shoe

19 St Christopher's Pl., W1 (B2)
☎ **020 7935 5589**
⊖ **Bond Street**
Mon.-Sat. 10am-6pm.
Thu. 10am-7pm.

This is the best place in London to buy smart, fashionable children's shoes. The stock includes both the usual brands and the company's own styles, as well as a few clothes (Paul Smith and Blu Kid.).

Humla

23 St Christopher's Pl., W1 (B2)
☎ **020 7224 1773**
⊖ **Bond Street**
Mon.-Sat. 10.30am-6.30pm.

Here you can dress your children from 0 to 8 years in lacy little frocks. Humla has its own label, including irresistible velvet dresses for £70, as well as the harder-wearing Oshkosh and Aztec ranges.

Laura Ashley Mother and Child

449-451 Oxford St., W1 (B2)
☎ **020 7355 1363**
⊖ **Marble Arch**
Mon.-Tue. and Sat. 10am-6.30pm, Wed. and Fri. 10am-7pm, Thu. 10am-8pm, Sun noon-6pm.

You'll find a range of clothes for babies and little girls (little boys are more or less ignored), in a similar vein to the designs on sale in the other Laura Ashley shops, in other words mostly pastel shades and pretty patterns of little flowers. Like this famous label's garments for adults, items for children are good quality and the prices not outrageous.

Young England

47 Elizabeth St., SW1 (B3)
☎ **020 7259 9003**
⊖ **Sloane Square**
Mon.-Fri. 10am-5.30pm, Sat. 10am-3pm.

This shop is the source of all the smocked dresses worn by the little girls of this smart area. Dressed in a blazer and shorts, your son will look as though he's ready for his first day at a public school. However, you'll certainly be paying a premium for these designer garments.

Patrizia Wigan

19 Walton St., SW3 (B3)
☎ 020 7823 7080
⊖ Knightsbridge
Mon.-Fri. 10am-6pm,
Sat. 10am-5.30pm.

Patrizia Wigan's line of
childrenswear combines classic
styles with a contemporary feel.
She uses very good quality fabrics,
and her velvet dresses with lace
collars and waxed parkas are the
last word in children's fashion.

Trotters

34 King's Rd, SW3 (A/B 3)
☎ 020 7259 9620
⊖ Sloane Square
Mon.-Fri. 9am-6.30pm, Wed.
9am-7pm Sat. 10am-6pm.

This is a shop to visit if you've
brought your children with you.
They can have their hair cut
without tears or screams – there's
an aquarium to keep them
amused during their ordeal.
There's also a very well-equipped
children's play area that you'll
have trouble tearing them away
from. If you've left them at home,
you can salve your conscience by
taking them back a selection of
the videos, books and toys that are
also on sale in
this shop.

Oilily

9 Sloane St., SW1 (B3)
☎ 020 7823 2505
⊖ Knightsbridge
Mon.-Sat. 10am-6pm, Wed.
10am-7pm. Sun. noon-4pm.

Brightly-coloured fabrics,
magnificent patchwork dresses
and denim jackets for the little
ones, in other words everything to
please both you and your children.
Of course none of this comes
cheap. Winter dresses start at £80,
summer dresses at £60.

Benjamin Pollock's Toy Shop

44 The Market, WC2 (C2)
☎ 020 7379 7866
⊖ Covent Garden
Mon.-Sat. 10.30am-6pm,
Sun. noon-5pm.

You have to go upstairs to reach
the treasures on sale in this little
shop – magnificent puppet
theatres, traditional teddy bears
and charming dolls. These are

toys for nostalgic adults and
careful children, but you can't go
far wrong if you stick to the
whistles, marbles and assorted
little figures, which are very pretty
and cost a lot less.

Children's clothes sizes are
given in terms of age (years
or months) and sometimes
height (for example 140 cm
(58 in) for a child of 10). If
you're not sure, always buy the
next size up. Children of 10
have quite often been known to
wear clothes designed to fit a
14-year-old. However much
you'd love to buy a pair of
classic children's shoes, it's not
a good idea unless the children
they're intended for are with
you, as their feet need to be
carefully measured for size
and width.

Daisy and Tom

181 King's Rd, SW3 (A/B3)
☎ 020 7352 5000
⊖ Sloane Square
Mon.-Fri. 10am-6pm,
Wed. 10am-7pm, Sat. 10am-
6.30pm, Sun. noon-6pm.

Take your children to this shop
with its wonderful merry-go-
round. Beautiful toys to suit every
pocket, a very good bookshop,
which even has a guide to
bringing up your tamagochi (£7),
and the Sodabar where your
children can slake their thirst.
They'll be planning your next
visit on the way out.

DEPARTMENT STORES

There are lots of reasons why you should take a wander round the department stores. Firstly, they sell almost every item you could dream of taking home from London, from souvenirs to cashmere, crockery and tea, all under one roof. Secondly, you won't find such fine quality anywhere else in the world. Watch out for the prices, though, as these can be higher than in the smaller shops. Although the sales give you a chance to make substantial savings, be prepared to fight your way through the crowds they attract.

Harrods

87-135 Brompton Rd., SW1 (A3)
☎ 020 7730 1234
Ⓔ Knightsbridge
Mon.-Tue. 10am-6pm
Wed.- Fri. 10am-7pm
Sat, 10am-6pm.

Harrods isn't just a department store, it's the most mythical of stores and a mecca for the compulsive shopper. It has extensive fashion departments, but you should go primarily for tableware, toys, and

the staggering range of watches on the ground floor. The enormous Food Hall, with its multicoloured tiles decorated with motifs of fish, game, vegetables and so on, is something that should on no account be missed. Remember, though, that you have to follow the rules. Don't think you'll be allowed in munching a hamburger. You must also be decently dressed and carry your rucksack in your arms. Sadly, photos aren't permitted.

Liberty

210-220 Regent St., W1 (B2)
☎ 020 7734 1234
Ⓔ Oxford Circus
Mon.-Wed. 10am-6.30pm,
Thu. 10am-8pm. Fri.-Sat 10am-7pm.

In the magnificent wood-panelled, Tudor-style interior of this store, you'll find traditions have been maintained. The famous

Liberty floral prints are on display in

every conceivable form, from (affordable) handkerchiefs to (impossibly expensive) sofas, but you can also simply buy the fabric by the metre, from £30 metre/39 in, all 137 cm/ 54 in wide. Liberty also has a magnificent selection of porcelain and china, including Wedgwood and Waterford. Their very popular sales take place in January and at the end of June.

Fortnum and Mason's

181 Piccadilly, W1 (B2)
☎ 020 7734 8040
Ⓔ Piccadilly Circus
Mon.-Sat. 9.30am-6pm.

This is the store for all those who love food. All the finest elements of British food are here, in a very warm and pleasant interior. If you'd like to sit down for a while, have a snack in the café on the 4th floor (see p. 37) or in the Fountain restaurant on the ground floor.

Peter Jones

Sloane Square, SW1 (B3)
☎ **020 7730 3434**
⊖ **Sloane Square**
Mon.-Sat. 9.30am-6pm,
Wed. 9.30am-7pm.

Once inside, keep going past the china, men's and women's fashions, gifts, furniture and accessories (this may prove tricky!) until you get to the café on the top floor. From here you'll have one of the best possible views over London. Take a break and enjoy.

Harvey Nichols

109-125 Knightsbridge,
SW1 (A3)
☎ **020 7235 5000**
⊖ **Knightsbridge**
Mon.-Tue. and Sat. 10am-

7pm, Wed.-Fri 10am-8pm,
Sun noon-6pm.

A shop devoted to stylish fashions and international designer labels. Everything from Lanvin, Christian Lacroix, Moschino and Versace to Calvin Klein and Dolce Gabbana underwear, or a little something from John Galliano. London's most up-to-the-minute store and a way of life. They have a household department, and a classy Food Hall and restaurants on the fifth floor.

Marks & Spencer

458 Oxford St., W1 (B2)
☎ **020 7935 7954**
⊖ **Marble Arch**
Mon.-Fri. 9am-8pm,
Sat. 9am-7pm,
Sun. noon-6pm.

This store is the famous chain's London flagship. In the food department, you'll find delicious take-away food, from sandwiches and salads to cottage cheese and Indian snacks, just what you need to eat on the hoof for as little as £1.50 (see p. 54). They'll give you plastic cutlery at the checkout. Oh, yes, and they do excellent clothes, too.

John Lewis

278-306 Oxford St., W1 (B2)
☎ **020 7629 7711**
⊖ **Oxford Circus**
Mon.-Wed. and Fri. 9.30am-
6pm, Thu. 10am-8pm,
Sat. 9am-6pm.

PERSONAL SHOPPING

This service, offered by some of the large stores, is intended to help you do your shopping. In some cases a member of the sales staff will come to your home, take a look at your wardrobe and help you make a list of everything you need to add to it. Shortly afterwards the clothes felt to be lacking will be delivered to your door for you to try.

You can also have a simplified version of this highly personalised service. All it takes is one phone call and you can have clothes delivered to your hotel for you to try. The stores that offer this 'personal grooming' service include:

Harvey Nichols
(by appointment,
☎ 020 7259 6638).
Free personalised advice service for both men and women, the rooms for trying clothes are provided with showers and refreshments.

Selfridge's
(by appointment
☎ 020 7318 3536)
Even at times when the store is closed, including Sunday, your Selfridge's consultant, or a member of her team, will interview you to identify your needs and bring you a choice of clothes to try, wherever you are in London, day or night. You're under no obligation to buy. What more could anyone ask?

The haberdashery department has an astounding range, from buttons to ribbons, and their dress fabric and home furnishing departments are wonderful too. This store is much loved for its high quality, unbeatable prices and their slogan 'never knowingly undersold'!.

HOME DECORATION

It can be a great idea to use your weekend in London as an opportunity to think about how to change the decoration of your home, particularly where the wallpaper and furnishings are concerned. British TV is swamped with shows about making over your decor in five seconds flat, but there's no substitute for looking for your wallpaper or fabric yourself. There are specialist shops for just about everything. from bell-pulls to baths and basins.

The Irish Linen Company

35-36 Burlington Arcade, W1 (B2)
☎ **020 7493 8949**
⊖ **Piccadilly Circus**
Mon.-Fri. 9.15am-5.30pm, Sat. 10am-5pm.

Here you'll find the finest and most durable sheets in the world, the kind that get passed down from mother to daughter. Prices are high (£345 for a pair of large linen sheets, to which you can add £47 for a pillow case of the same quality), but there's nothing

to stop you buying only a fine linen hankie or two (£3.50-£12). The shop's retro interior is worth a visit in itself.

Smallbone of Devizes

105-109 Fulham Rd, SW3 (A3)
☎ **020 7581 9989**
⊖ **South Kensington**
Mon.-Fri. 9am-5.30pm, Sat. 10am-5pm, Sun, noon-6pm.

Contemporary and classic furniture from bedroom to kitchen plus furnishings and upholstery fabrics. Everything here is made-to-measure or adapted to suit your needs. Ideal if you want to give your flat a new look. Prices reflect

the upmarket area but items can be shipped abroad.

The Linen Merchant

11 Montpellier St., SW7 (A3)
☎ **020 7584 3654**
⊖ **Knightsbridge**
Mon.-Sat. 9.30am-6pm.

Only fine linens are sold in this lavender-scented shop – sheets for dreamers (£60 for a set for a child's bed), tablecloths for great occasions (£900!) and charming nightdresses (£40+). Items can be embroidered with the client's own monogram.

Christopher Wray

199 Shaftesbury Ave, WC2 (B1-2)
☎ **020 7437 6199**
⊖ **Tottenham Court Rd**
Mon.-Sat. 10am-6pm, Thu. 9.30am-7pm.

If you like contemporary lighting, you'll love the rails supporting spotlights shaped like slender swallows. Beautiful copies of lamps by Charles Rennie Macintosh, the architect of the British Art Nouveau movement.

Designers Guild

267-272 Kings Rd, SW3 (A3)
☎ 020 7351 5775
⊖ South Kensington
Mon.-Tue. 9.30am-5.30pm,
Wed.-Sat 10am-6pm,
Sun. noon-5pm.

One of the first high-street design shops with a difference. Designers Guild is noted for its strong, vibrantly coloured wallpapers and fabrics – there's a collection of over 2,000. An ideal place to get some new ideas or take advantage of the interior design service. The stock changes constantly but always offers a selection of furniture, bedlinen, ceramics, lighting and kitchenware. You can relax with a foamy cappuccino in the café.

Laura Ashley

7-9 Harriet St., SW1 (A3)
☎ 020 7235 9797
⊖ Knightsbridge
Mon.-Fri. 10am-6pm,
Sat. 9.30am-6pm.

Turn your home into an English garden with the flowery wallpapers and furnishing fabrics from this branch, which is entirely devoted to their home decoration range. Prices are reasonable (lovely designs for as little as £8 for a roll of wallpaper).

The Conran Shop

81 Fulham Rd, SW3 (A3)
☎ 020 7589 7401
⊖ South Kensington
Mon.-Tue. and Fri. 10am-6pm, Wed.-Thu. 10am-7pm, Sat. 10am-6.30pm, Sun. noon-6pm.

Sir Terence Conran founded Habitat in the 60s before opening his Conran Shops in London and abroad. Here you'll find innovative designers, buyers who scour the world for interesting objects and the creative team behind Conran's own brand, all helping you bring a new originality to your home, with Indian doorways, moulded beech chairs, fabrics, linen, crockery and bathroom accessories. Be sure to visit the Fulham Road shop, home to the Michelin showrooms in the early 20th century, which is like a contemporary design gallery.

The Inventory

16-40 Kensington High St., W8 (A3)
☎ 020 937 2626
⊖ High Street Kensington
Mon.-Sat. 10am-7pm, Sun. noon-6pm.

Bright, 'now' homeware over three floors stacked high and sold cheap. Cups, plates, teapots and kitchenware on the ground floor, bed-linen, towels and ready-made curtains on the first and lighting in the basement. Lots of fun, easy-living ideas.

Jerry's Home Store

163-167 Fulham Rd, SW6 (A3)
☎ 020 7581 0909
⊖ South Kensington
Mon.-Tue. and Fri. 10am-6pm, Wed.-Thu. 10am-7pm, Sat. 10am-6.30pm, Sun 11.30am-5.30pm.

A celebration of American culinary culture. From popcorn-makers to plates that wouldn't look out of place in any diner, the design mingles the pop and popular with the more downhome traditional. The 'animal' range includes spangly bowls for your old hound-dog, or try the *Friends* cookbook if you'd like to sample recipes from the stars of your favourite sitcom.

WALLPAPER

If you want to buy wallpaper, make sure you bring with you the exact dimensions of the room you're intending to paper, in other words the total length of all the walls and their height from floor to ceiling. Find out all you can about the quality of the paper: if it hasn't been 'coated', it will absorb cigarette smoke and dust and won't last much beyond five years. Unfortunately, this is often true of Laura Ashley papers; however this brand also does excellent vinyl wallpapers that are perfect for the kitchen. Lastly, don't forget to check out the borders that you can buy to match your wallpaper, which will give your room the final, finishing touch.

SILVER AND JEWELLERY

Kings of Sheffield

319 Regent St., W1 (B2)
☎ 020 7637 9888
⊖ Oxford Circus
Mon.-Sat. 10am-6pm.

Kings of Sheffield is a famous name in cutlery. It gives great value for money and all, or almost all, the available styles are available in three qualities of silver. Two are silver plate, the third sterling silver, also known as plain silver. For a 44-piece dining service you should allow £846 for the best quality silver plate (guaranteed for life, apparently) and £2,500 for the same service in sterling silver.

London Silver Vaults

Chancery House,
53-63 Chancery Lane,
WC2 (B2)
☎ 020 7242 3844
⊖ Chancery Lane
Mon.-Fri. 9am-5.30pm,
Sat. 9am-1pm.

A trip to the London Silver Vaults is a real adventure. You go down a long, rather dimly-lit staircase, wondering if you've got the wrong address, then through a few heavy security doors until you arrive at last in the holy of holies of London silver. The best stall for small, cheap (£5) pieces is David Shure, a great place to find little gifts. One of the finest stalls, Feldman's, has exceptional pieces on show costing thousands of pounds. Rather disconcertingly, the walls behind the forty stands have been decorated in exactly the same shade of blue as the insides of the cases on which the silver is displayed.

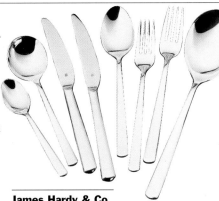

James Hardy & Co

235 Brompton Rd, SW3 (A3)
☎ 020 7586 5050
⊖ South Kensington
Mon.-Sat. 10am-5pm.

Full of silver and jewellery, every piece rare and utterly magnificent, this antique dealer's superb window display can't fail to catch your eye. A shop with a long history, it was established in 1853.

M P Levene

5 Thurloe Pl., SW7 (A3)
☎ 020 7589 3744
⊖ South Kensington
Mon.-Fri. 9am-6pm,
Sat. 9am-1pm.

English antique silverware, and you can even commission a silver model of your yacht.

Angela Hale

5 The Royal Arcade,
28 Old Bond St.,
W1 (B2)
☎ 020 7495 1920
www.angelahale.co.uk
⊖ Green Park
Mon.-Sat. 10am-6pm.

Art Deco and clip-on 1950s pieces, hairclips and wedding tiaras for the fashion junkie look. This is the place where fashion gurus and supermodels come to find that quirky, individual piece. Vintage handbags upstairs to complete the look.

CHINA AND PORCELAIN

Thomas Goode & Co

19 South Audley St., W1 (B2)
☎ **020 7499 2823**
⊖ **Green Park**
Mon.-Sat. 10am-6pm.

The advantage of this large store is that it sells all the big names in china and silver. The marble columns of its immense façade give little idea of its vast sales floor and upmarket status. Everything here is expensive (from £32 for a pretty china plate), though no more than elsewhere for the same quality.

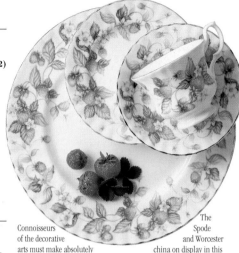

Waterford Wedgwood

173-174 Piccadilly, W1 (B2)
☎ **020 7629 2614**
⊖ **Piccadilly Circus**
Mon.-Fri. 9am-6pm,
Sat. 9.30-6pm.

Besides the neo-Classical design of blue Wedgwood china, you'll find plenty of high-quality tableware in this shop. Since they teamed up with Waterford, they also have a collection of elegant crystal.

Connoisseurs of the decorative arts must make absolutely certain to step inside this shop. Its porcelain figurines are among the most famous in the world. It also has the advantage of being considerably cheaper than its rival Wedgwood. Of course that's relatively speaking, since twenty-four plates – twelve 27cm/ 10½in in diameter and twelve 20cm/7½in in diameter – will still set you back between £500 and £1200, depending on the style.

The Spode and Worcester china on display in this shop is not only a little simpler, but also noticably cheaper than the wares in the previous two stores. It's certainly worth your attention, if only for the variety of the decoration, from the most everyday ranges to some very fine floral designs. You should expect to pay about £400 for an ordinary 24-piece service and at least £1,000 for a bone china service of the same size.

Royal Doulton

167 Piccadilly, W1 (B2)
☎ **020 7493 9121**
⊖ **Piccadilly Circus**
Mon.-Sat. 9.30am-6pm.

Chinacraft

137 Regent St., W1 (B2)
☎ **020 7734 3076**
⊖ **Piccadilly Circus**

LOOKING AFTER YOUR PORCELAIN

Bone china shouldn't be washed in the dishwasher. Wash it carefully by hand using nothing but washing-up liquid. Don't put your plates in the microwave, particularly if they're decorated with gold as they'll spark, and don't subject them to sudden temperature changes. If you have old plates or dishes, try not to use them for juicy red fruits or anything that you eat with French dressing, like salads. The liquid from these will penetrate any tiny superficial cracks in the glaze and leave a stain, spoiling the colour of your crockery.

ANTIQUES

London is without doubt one of the most important centres in the world when it comes to the antiques market, particularly because of the famous auction houses which have been established here for generations. If you know what you're looking for and are prepared to pay the price to acquire that special piece your collection lacks, you'll be in paradise.

If not, don't expect to find any great bargains, as prices can be high, particularly if you have to take the cost of transportation into consideration.

Admiral Vernon

141-149 Portobello Rd, W11 (off map)
☎ 020 7727 5242
⊖ **Notting Hill Gate**
Sat. 5am-5pm.

This elegant market, located a little away from the more tourist-filled streets of Portobello, attracts connoisseurs and even the odd professional buyer, who come to hunt through the ornaments, china, fashion accessories and jewellery from the late 19th and early 20th centuries. A good place to find unusual souvenirs at prices that aren't too high.

John Jesse

160 Kensington Church St., W8 (off map)
☎ 020 7229 0312
⊖ **Notting Hill Gate**
Mon.-Fri. 10am-5pm,
Sat. 11am-3pm.

John Jesse specialises in Art Nouveau. Here connoisseurs will find a few pieces of furniture and lots of beautiful china and silver, as well as jewellery and Mucha posters. This shop is one of the best of its kind, but no prices are shown and the owner is about as friendly as a bear with a sore head.

Bond Street Silver Gallery

111-112 New Bond St., W1 (B2)
☎ 020 7493 6180
⊖ **Bond Street**
Mon.-Fri. 9am-5.30pm.

The three floors and seventeen stands in this antiques market are entirely devoted to silver and jewellery. It's a prestigious establishment with high prices and the sales staff make sure you're aware of the fact.

TO BUY OR NOT TO BUY...

You haven't got a lot of time, certainly not enough to go round all the shops comparing prices, and you've got to make a quick decision. Before you do something silly, ask yourself a few common-sense questions:

■ Is it the sort of item aimed at tourists that you'll find a lot cheaper three streets further on (particularly in the case of sweaters and tartans)?
■ Are you sure you can't get exactly the same thing at home?
■ Are you sure you can get it more cheaply here than at home (this is a particularly important question if you've got to pay to have it sent home. Find out what the transportation costs will be beforehand).
■ Lastly, if you do spend a fortune on a whim, on a pair of shoes, for example, or a silver dinner service, you'll at least have the pleasure of taking something home that will always have the added value of the memories associated with it, and those are beyond price.

Retro Home

**20 Pembridge Rd, W11
(off map)
☎ 020 7221 2055
⊖ Notting Hill Gate
Open every day 10am-8pm.**

Don't hesitate to rummage through the items on display in the window of this bric-a-brac shop. Ornaments, old toys (Dinky Toys and Snoopys) and crockery are classified by price. Most items are between £1 and £20, so don't hold back. There are also some formica tables (yes, it's back in fashion!).

Gray's Antique Market

**58 Davies St., W1 (B2)
☎ 020 7629 7034
⊖ Bond Street
Mon.-Fri. 10am-6pm.**

Also of interest in this market, besides the antiques on sale, of course, is the rather odd fact that it has a river running through it (the Tyburn, in the basement) – you can even have a bite to eat sitting beside it. It's mostly

crockery and silver on sale here, as well as antiques from around the world.

Eskanazi

**10 Clifford St., W1 (B2)
☎ 020 7493 5464
⊖ Piccadilly Circus
Mon.-Fri. 9.30am-5.30pm.**

Real connoisseurs of ivory should rush to this dealer's, where they'll find one of the finest collections of netsuke in Europe. There's no hope of finding anything under £1,000 here but the artistry of the craftsmanship is superb.

Alfie's Antique Market

**13-25 Church St., NW8 (A1)
☎ 020 7723 6066
⊖ Edgware Road
Tue.-Sat. 10am-6pm.**

Four floors filled with all kinds of antiques (jewellery, furniture, lamps and paintings). This is one of the best-stocked shops in London and a real paradise for bargain-hunters.

The Map House

**54 Beauchamp Pl., SW3 (A3)
☎ 020 7589 4325
⊖ Knightsbridge
Mon.-Fri. 9.45am-5.45pm,
Sat. 10.30am-5pm.**

This shop, with its four show-rooms, is entirely devoted to maps. From the documents on display, some of which date back to the 17th century, you can get some idea of just how large the British Empire was.

Gallery of Antique Costume and Textiles

**2 Church St., W1 (A1)
☎ 020 7723 9981
⊖ Marylebone
Mon.-Sat. 10am-5.30pm.**

Here there's fabric everywhere – silks, satin, velvet and chenille – on the walls, ceiling and floor, with costumes from the 1920s and 30s downstairs. Luxuriate!

FOOD AND DRINK

British cooking has suffered from a pretty poor press over the years, but there have been enormous shifts in British attitudes to eating. The cult of the celebrity TV chef reflects that revolution and British chefs regularly gain international awards. In London you can find cuisine from seventy different countries and traditional British cuisine has a new, fresh style.

Tesco Metro

22 Bedford St., WC2 (C2)
☎ **020 7853 7500**
⊖ **Covent Garden**
Mon.-Fri. 8am-10pm,
Sat. 7.30am-10pm,
Sun. noon-6pm.

Not so much a supermarket, more a way of London life. For some years, Tesco has been winning the battle of the supermarkets, and this is typical of their city centre stores where you can satisfy all your domestic needs,

from washing powder and cleaning products, to catering for a smart dinner party from their

prepared foods. Excellent fresh sandwiches for a meal on the hoof.

Planet Organic

42 Westbourne Gr., W2 (A2)
☎ **020 7221 7171**
⊖ **Bayswater**
22 Torrington Pl., WC1
⊖ **Goodge Street.**
Mon.-Sat. 9am-8pm,
Sun. 11am-5pm.

Vegetarian supermarkets, an idea imported from the USA, are now starting to proliferate in Europe. This is a perfect example of the genre. All the products are guaranteed free of pesticides and artificial fertilizers. The fruits and vegetables have that natural, individual look, and you can restore your energies with a carrot and ginger juice at the bar.

TEA AND COFFEE

Algerian Coffee Store

52 Old Compton St., W1 (C2)
☎ **020 7437 2480**
⊖ **Leicester Square**
Mon.-Sat. 9am-7pm.

Don't be fooled by the name.

This little shop is a favourite haunt of many Londoners, who come here to buy their tea and coffee. Inside,

the shop is crammed with all the gadgets to do with tea. You'll find teas flavoured with your favourite fruit, as well as good old darjeeling and green tea. The range of coffees is spectacular, too.

Whittards

209 Kensington High St., W8
(off map)
☎ **020 7938 4344.**
⊖ **High Street Kensington**
Mon.-Sat. 10am-7pm,
Sun. noon-6pm.

This shop is one of the many branches of Whittards you'll come across in your walks round the city. It's only very recently that the shops have multiplied in this way after a century of peaceful activity in Chelsea. They sell classic teas and rarer ones from single plantations alongside the very popular fruit teas. They also have a wide selection of equally exotic coffees, as well as cheerful china mugs and teapots.

H. R Higgins

79 Duke St., W1 (B2)
☎ **020 7491 8819**
⊖ **Bond Street**
Mon.-Wed. 8.45am-5.30pm,
Thu.-Fri. 8.45am-6pm,
Sat. 10am-5pm.

This shop, ideally situated not too far from Piccadilly Circus, supplies excellent teas. You can also buy coffee here from all the best sources (about £4.40 for 500g/1lb of Kenyan coffee).

DON'T FORGET THE CLASSICS.

Essential purchases for visitors from abroad include a jar of Marmite (yeast extract spread), bitter orange marmalade and lemon curd (made from egg yolks and lemon juice), which you'll need if you want to recreate the great British teatime experience at home. Connoisseurs of exotic flavours would be well advised to slip in a jar of apple, mango or lime chutney (sweet and spicy condiment) as well – it's lovely with chicken. Powdered mustard (Coleman's Mustard), much stronger than its American, French or German cousins, will please those who love powerful tastes. Lastly, take home some British cheese from Neal's Yard Dairies, 17 Shorts Gdns, Covent Garden. It generally travels well.

tea), and a museum in which you can explore the history of what has become a British institution.

CHEESES

Neal's Yard Dairy

17 Shorts Gardens, WC2 (C2)
☎ 020 7379 7646.
⊖ Covent Garden
Mon.-Sat. 9am-7pm,
Sun. 10am-5pm.

If British cheeses other than cheddar are now popular again, it's partly thanks to the passionate support they've received from the owners of this shop. To encourage you to share their enthusiasm, they give you a sliver to taste before you buy. They also sell Sally Clarke bread (see p. 45).

WHISKY

Bloomsbury Wine Company

3 Bloomsbury St., WC1 (C1)
☎ 020 7436 4763
⊖ Tottenham Court Road
Mon.-Fri. 9.30am-5.30pm.

This shop has an enormous selection of whiskies from a great many different manufacturers. They stock bottles of 18 year-old Glenmorangie. Anything you buy can be delivered abroad.

Cadenhead's Covent Garden Whisky shop

3 Russell St., WC2 (C2)
☎ 020 7379 4640
⊖ Covent Garden
Mon. and Sat. 11am-6.30pm,
Tue.-Fri. 11am-4.30pm,
Sun. noon-4.30pm.

They take whisky seriously here. Over 200 different malts and blends from all over Scotland, and a good selection of Irish whiskey.

R. Twining and Co

216 Strand, WC2 (C2)
☎ 020 7353 3511
⊖ Temple
Mon.-Fri. 9.30am-4.45pm.

The golden lion above the entrance is a reminder that the shop first opened on this very spot in 1717. Inside you'll find all the teas sold by variety (from £1 for 125g/4oz of English Breakfast

Paxton & Whitfield

93 Jermyn St., SW1 (B2)
☎ 020 7930 0259
⊖ Piccadilly Circus
Mon.-Fri. 9.30am-6pm,
Sat. 9am-5.30pm.

This shop opened in 1797. The walls of its long interior are covered in cheese from around the world, as well as delicious English hams and preserves.

MARKETS

London's markets are like open-air Ali Baba's caves. In these city bazaars you'll find everything from antiques and secondhand clothes to arts and crafts and organic foods. A visit to one of the food markets (selling both British staples and more exotic produce) is the simplest way of rubbing shoulders with real Londoners, but don't forget to check opening days and times before setting off.

Berwick Street Market

**Berwick St. and
Rupert St., W1 (C2)
⊖ Leicester Square
Mon.-Sat. 9am-6pm.**

This is one of the few markets in the West End selling ordinary food, and it's the perfect place to buy cheese and fruit. You can also drop

into the sausage shop **Simply Sausages** (see p. 49), which you'll find in the middle of the market

Spitalfields Market

**Commercial St., E1
(off map)
⊖ Liverpool Street
Fri. and Sun. 9am-3pm.**

Spitalfields is an organic market held in an enormous hall that also houses a sports centre. All the food on sale is guaranteed to have been produced without the use of

nitrates or pesticides, and the current vogue for organic products means this is a trendy place to be on a Sunday morning.

Leadenhall Market

**Whittington Ave, EC3
(off map)
⊖ Bank
Mon.-Fri. 7am-4pm.**

In Sir Horace Jones's magnificent Victorian market hall you'll still find the odd stall selling game (sold on this site in season since the Middle Ages), fish and cheese, but tacky clothes and souvenirs are gradually taking over. Best visited on a weekday morning, when it's full of workers from the City sipping their espressos as they read the newspaper.

Brixton Market

**Electric Ave, Pope's Rd, SW9
(off map)
⊖ Brixton
Mon.-Tue. and Thu.-Sat.
8.30am-5.30pm,
Wed. 8.30am-1pm.**

This is the most disorientating market in London, with many of the stalls selling products from Africa and the Caribbean representative of the origins of the many different communities living in Brixton. Shoppers queueing to buy plantains, goat's meat or sweet potatoes are serenaded by reggae and calypso sounds from the music stalls. Lots of very cheap secondhand clothes. An experience not to be missed.

Jubilee and Apple Markets

Jubilee Hall and The Piazza, Covent Garden, WC2 (C2)
⊖ Covent Garden
Open every day 9am-5pm.

These two markets are patronised by tourists as they're located in the heart of Covent Garden. Antiques on Monday, crafts at the weekend and a more general market the rest of the week. It's a good place to find souvenirs and little gifts.

Portobello Road Market

Portobello Rd, W10 (off map)
⊖ Notting Hill Gate
Sat. 7am-5.30pm.

The market is north of the tube station, off Pembridge Road, in trendy Notting Hill. It soon becomes crowded in fine weather, but there are some interesting, original stalls. Beware – the prices are set for tourists and rise with the temperature. Further down you'll find secondhand clothes, gadgets and a food market that opens on Fridays as well.

Camden Market

Camden Lock, Buck St., Electric Ballroom, Chalk Farm Rd and Commercial Pl., NW1 (off map)
⊖ Camden Town
Mon.-Fri. 9.30am-5.30pm, Sat.-Sun. 10am-6pm.

Over the years Camden Market has become a major attraction for a young clientele and is what's generally known as a flea market. In this New Age mecca you'll find secondhand clothes, crafts, vegetarian restaurants and a stall dealing in legal herbs that

supposedly have the same effects as their illegal counterparts!

Brick Lane Market

Brick Lane and surrounding area, E2 (off map)
⊖ Shoreditch
Sun. 6am-1pm.

You'll find a mixture of food and bric-a-brac in this very popular East End market, which is patronised only by real Londoners. It's one of the Sunday meeting places of London's Indian and Asian communities. So forget the stereotypes and get to grips with authentic London and its inhabitants.

HAGGLING IN THE MARKETS

It's not always easy to get the price of an object or piece of furniture down when you're actually standing in front of a stall in the flea market, but it might be worth bearing in mind some basic tips. For example, you should never ask 'How much is it?' as you would in a traditional shop, but try instead, 'What do you want for it?', or 'What's your best price?', indicating that what you want to pay for it might be different and that you're intending to haggle. Generally speaking you ought to be able to get the price down by at least 10%.

DISCOUNT AND SECONDHAND SHOPS

Like most great capitals, London is an expensive place to live, but Londoners have developed a few ways to cope. Visits to the discount, charity and secondhand shops have now become indispensable, and no one is ashamed to be seen sifting through their wares. So when in London, do as the locals do and make sure you call in on some of these shops. You're bound to save yourself a bit of money and you may find some really amazing bargains.

Browns Labels for Less

50 South Molton St., W1 (B2)
☎ 020 7491 7833
⊖ **Bond Street**
Mon. 11am-6.30pm, Tue.-Fri. 11am-7pm, Sat. 11am-6.30pm, Sun. noon-4.30pm.

Last year's collections from British and international designers (Gigli, Missoni and Comme des Garçons), sold at half their original price. More affordable than in the designer shops, but not that cheap all the same. Good range of men's fashions, which is quite rare.

TK Maxx

Drumond Centre, North End, Croydon, Surrey (off map)
☎ 020 8686 9753
Rail E. or W. Croydon from Charing Cross or Victoria
Mon.-Fri. 9am-6pm, Thu. 9am-9pm, Sun. 11am-5pm.

This big store has collections from all the current big-name designers. Armani, Saint-Laurent, Calvin Klein, Nicole Farhi and co. are all represented at extraordinary prices. They're really slashed, often by as much as 50%. To take advantage of these bargains you'll have to take a train from London Bridge or Victoria station, as this shop isn't in central London, but, with prices like these it's worth, the effort.

Paul Smith

23 Avery Row, W1 (B2)
☎ 020 7493 1287
⊖ **Bond Street**
Mon.-Wed. and Fri.-Sat. 10am-6.30pm, Thu. 10am-7pm.

This is where the designer sells off his creations, with some great reductions (see p. 58).

Burberry Factory Shop

29-53 Chatham Pl., E9 (off map)
☎ 020 8985 3344
Buses 22A, 22B, 48, 55, 253 and 277
Mon.-Fri. 11am-6pm, Sat. 10am-4.30pm, Sun. 11am-5pm.

Don't expect to find the celebrated macs at half price, but there are plenty of classic garments at bargain prices. The shop isn't exactly a well-kept secret, so expect to see coachloads of tourists, but there's plenty for everyone.

Oxfam Originals

26 Ganton St., W1 (B2)
☎ 020 7437 7338
⊖ **Oxford Circus**
Mon.-Sat. 11am-6pm.

One of *the* brilliant charity shops. This is the Oxfam retro shop, where anything worth salvaging for today's groovsters is cleaned and recycled to emerge as the coolest thing on the street.

In-Wear

100 Garratt Lane, SW19 (off map)
☎ 020 8871 2155
Rail Earsfield
Mon.-Sat. 10am-5.30pm.

In-Wear have been around for a while, but they've kept their style and identity. Here you'll find garments for both men and women from the ready-to-wear range at low prices. The discounts on men's clothes really repay the effort of getting here.

Amazon

1-22 Kensington Church St., W8 (off map)
No phone
⊖ **High Street Kensington**
Mon.-Sat. 10am-8pm.
Sun. noon-6pm.

Eleven floors of fashion in seven shops where the prices are slashed to ribbons. Each shop has a different atmosphere. Slinky, silky Fenn Wright Mansion separates, soft Nicole Farhi outfits and funky French Connection. There's a men's department and shoes for kids. The sales are awesome.

Discount Dressing

39 Paddington St., W1 (off map)
☎ 020 7486 7230
⊖ **Baker Street**
Mon.-Sun. 10am-6pm.

This discount shop sells clothes by the greatest European designers at reductions of 50-90% of the usual prices. With deals like that on offer, you'd be hard put to find something selling for less elsewhere. If you do manage to, Discount Dressing will refund the difference. Cheap and fair.

SECONDHAND

Pop Boutique

6 Monmouth St., WC2 (C2)
☎ 020 7497 5262
⊖ **Covent Garden**
Mon.-Sat. 11am-7pm,
Sun. noon-5pm.

Pop as in Pop Art or Pop Music, with an emphasis on the 1970s. Secondhand clothes and old stock, particularly jeans, for you to reconstruct a complete seventies look. Beloved of London students for its reasonable prices. They also sell electrical goods like retro radios and even some magnficent toasters.

Yesterday's Bread

29 Foubert's Pl., W1 (B2)
☎ **020 7287 1929**
⊖ **Oxford Circus**
Mon.-Fri. 11.30am-6.30pm,
Sat. 11am-6pm.

The psychedelic window display says it all. Here you'll find everything you need to act the part of a Beatles fan from the days of 'Lucy in the Sky with Diamonds', T-shirts with hallucinatory designs, 'made in Woodstock' skirts and even period postcards of your favourite groups.

Laurence Corner

62-64 Hampstead Rd, NW1 (off map)
☎ **020 7813 1010**
⊖ **Warren Street**
Mon.-Sat. 9.30am-6pm.

Fans of American army surplus clothing will love this store. Everything from T-shirts to military-style jackets and dungarees, with generally cheap prices. To hunt down a real bargain though, you have to put the time in.

Dolly Diamond

51 Pembridge Road, W11 (off map)
☎ **020 7792 2479**
⊖ **Notting Hill Gate**
Mon.-Fri. 10.30am-6.30pm,
Sat. 9.30am-6.30pm.
Sun. noon-6pm.

After a period of closure, Dolly Diamond has opened once more,

to the great relief of Londoners. From retro to 1980s styles, this is the place to seek out secondhand clothing that's both elegant and very good quality, like a sequin-trimmed evening gown. If your find needs a bit of patching up, the shop will do it for you.

Sheila Cook

184 Westbourne Grove, W11 (off map)
☎ **020 7792 8001**
www.sheilacook.co.uk
⊖ **Notting Hill Gate**
Tue.-Wed. by appointment.
Thu.-Sat. 10am-6pm.

The antique clothes in this elegant shop are personally selected by the owner and sold in tiptop condition. Rare items from 1760 to 1960, plus lots of accessories and fabrics.

The Charity Shop

211 Brompton Rd, SW7 (A3)
☎ **020 7581 7987**
⊖ **South Kensington**
Mon.-Sat. 10am-6pm,
Sun. noon-4pm.

This is one of the many charity shops in London. It has the merit of being supplied from the

THE ART OF BUYING SECONDHAND

Buying clothes that someone else has worn, even of the most ordinary kind, is common practice nowadays. The growth of charity shops responds both to the needs of their customers – secondhand clothes are cheaper than new ones – and fund-raising, since the money goes to various good causes. A whole culture has grown up around secondhand clothes: designers use them as a source of ideas, while the young, hip and trendy create original looks on the cheap from old uniforms or granny's dresses. All it takes is a bit of luck and imagination. It's up to you.

wardrobes of local residents, so it regularly has very good quality clothes, sometimes from big name labels, for a maximum of £25.

Sue Ryder

122 Wigmore St., W1 (B2)
☎ 020 7224 1563
⊖ Bond Street
Mon.-Sat. 10am-5pm.

Don't be put off by the rather uninspiring window display. On a good day you can find real treasures that have been cast off by the inhabitants of this wealthy district. What's available varies

from day to day, depending on who's turned out their wardrobe, but it's always worth calling in. You might find the perfect dress or even a bijou designer item, all at knockdown prices.

Vent

178a Westbourne Grove, W11 (entrance on Ledbury Rd, off map)
No telephone
⊖ Notting Hill Gate
Fri. and Sat. 11am-6pm.

This shop was opened by a secondhand enthusiast and professional architect, who has gradually built up an exceptional collection of clothes and accessories from various different periods and designers. All items on sale are original and prices vary widely.

L'Homme Designer Exchange

50 Blandfort St., W1 (B2)
☎ 020 7224 3261
⊖ Bond Street
Mon.-Thu. 11am-6pm,
Fri. 11.30am-6pm,
Sat. 11am-5pm.

You won't believe it! Designer suits for men at a third of the normal price: Paul Smith, Armani, Issaye Miyake – you name it, they've got it. With a prices of £180 instead of £500+, it's got to make sense.

Designer 2nd Hand Shop

24 Hampstead High St., NW3 (off map)
☎ 020 7431 8618
⊖ Hampstead
Mon.-Sun. 11am-6pm.

Lots of designer creations are re-sold at very low prices in this little Hampstead shop. All the clothes are in very good condition.

Cornucopia

12, Upper Tachbrook St., SW1 (B3)
☎ 020 7828 5752
⊖ Victoria
7 days a week, 11am-6pm.

An enormous choice of dresses dating from 1910 to 1960. Though they're not always in tiptop condition, they're certainly at the lowest prices. Give yourself plenty of time here, because you'll want to spend hours trying things on. There are loads of accessories too.

GIFTS

Forget the tourist traps full of tacky trinkets and trash made in Taiwan that you can find on every street corner, and seek out some of the less conventional places. The city is bursting with unusual shops where you'll have no trouble finding the ideal item that you could never buy back home. There are shops with weird, fun and even wild and outrageous gifts for you to take back as perfect souvenirs.

Janet Fitch

37A Neal St., WC2 (C2)
☎ 020 7240 6332
⊖ Covent Garden
Mon.-Sat. 11am-7pm,
Sun. 1-6pm.

This shop is just the place to find a lovely piece of jewellery for yourself or a friend without spending a fortune. The best young British designers are all represented. Their very varied and elegant creations are of silver and semi-precious stones (allow £30+ for a lovely ring).

Forbidden Planet

71-75 New Oxford St., WC1 (C2)
☎ 020 7836 4179
⊖ Tottenham Court Road
Mon.-Sat. 10am-6pm,
Thu.-Fri. 10am-7pm.

All your favourite heroes are here, from *The X-Files* to the *X-Men*, and from obscure comic heroes to *Superman*. This shop specialises in Underground comics, but you can get all the 'Wallace and Gromit' spin-off products here too.

Space NK

37 Earlham Street, WC2 (C2)
☎ 020 7379 7030
⊖ Covent Garden
Mon.-Fri. 10am-7pm, Thu.
10am-8pm, Sun 11am-5pm.

Never trust appearances. What you might think is a post-conceptual installation is in fact a shop selling beauty products. Snatch up the creams by Kiehl (from New

York – their distribution is fairly exclusive), Philosophy (for their amusing names) or the unbelievable colours from Antonia Flowers.

Stage & Screen

34 Notting Hill Gate, W11 (off map)
☎ 020 7221 3646
⊖ Notting Hill Gate
Open 7 days a week,
10am-8pm.

This shop boasts an impressive stock of items, all secondhand. Films and TV shows, books, memorabilia and some remarkable original posters.

The Museum Store

37, The Market, The Piazza, WC2 (C2)
☎ 020 7431 7156
⊖ Covent Garden
Mon.-Sat. 10am-6pm,
Sun. 11am-5pm.

Don't be surprised if you catch the Mona Lisa smiling secretively at you from a poster high on the wall. This shop sells reproductions of exhibits from museums all over the world, all under one roof, including gifts from the shops of the Victoria and Albert Museum and Tate Britain, all without having to do the rounds. Postcards 50p, posters from £4.

London Transport Museum Shop

The Piazza, Covent Garden, WC2 (C2)
☎ 020 7379 6344
⊖ Covent Garden
Mon.-Sun. 10am-6pm,
Fri. 11am-6pm.

The shop in the very entertaining London Transport Museum is fantastic, and there are thousands of gift ideas here, from the kitsch (a china model of an old-fashioned London bus), to the extraordinary (a beautiful book of photos of items left behind on tube trains), not to mention the most cryptic (a T-shirt printed with the

phrase 'mind the gap' – which can often be heard on the London Tube warning passengers as they get out of the train). An inexhaustible goldmine, and not at all expensive.

Penhaligon's
41 Wellington St., WC2 (C2)
☎ 020 7836 2150
⊖ Covent Garden
8 Cornhill, The Royal Exchange, EC3
☎ 020 7283 0711
⊖ Bank
Mon.-Fri. 10am-6pm. Sun. noon-5pm (not Cornhill).

Honour where it's due: Penhaligon's is the queen's official supplier of perfumes. You'll find all kinds of very British scents (the best known, 'Bluebell', costs £29.50 for 50 ml) and beauty products, all presented in beautiful Victorian-style bottles, which would make lovely gifts.

Crabtree & Evelyn
239 Regent St., W1 (B2)
☎ 020 7409 1603
⊖ Piccadilly Circus
Mon.-Wed. 10am-6.30pm,

Thu. 10am-8pm,
Fri.-Sat. 10am-6.30pm,
Sun. noon-5pm.

Another 'typically English' purveyor of perfumes, where, besides the classic scents, you can buy pot-pourri for the home, accessories, tea and china, all in very good taste and not at all expensive. The Evelyn classic lavender and rose soaps are wonderful, but they also have more exotic, oriental perfumes. The perfect shop to visit if you're short of ideas for classic gifts to take home.

John Gray
82B Portobello Rd, W11
(off map)
☎ 020 7229 2544
⊖ Notting Hill Gate
Mon.-Sat. 9.30am-5pm.

Take advantage of your trip to the Portobello market to visit this dealer in old luggage. All the items on sale here are so beautiful, you'd expect to find something belonging to Phileas Fogg.

Faxcessory
Embankment Pl.,
Villiers St., WC2 (C2)
☎ 020 7321 0074
⊖ Charing Cross
Mon.-Fri. 9.30am-7pm,
Sat. 10.30am-5.30pm.

The famous ring-bound Filofax personal organisers make gifts that are both useful and stylish. What's more, prices here

are keen and cheaper than overseas. There's a wide range of styles and accessories in this specialist shop. The original leather-bound organisers start at around £15.

James Smith & Sons

53 New Oxford St., WC1 (C2)
☎ 020 7836 4731
⊖ Tottenham Court Road
Mon.-Fri. 9.30am-5.30pm,
Sat. 10am-5.30pm.

Your trip to London may well give you a chance to appreciate the truth of the old adage, 'It never rains but it pours' but forewarned is forearmed – make sure you visit Smith & Sons. This venerable institution, trading from the same address since 1857, offers you umbrellas and made-to-measure walking sticks. You'll have no trouble finding just the right item among the impressive range on display, including the extraordinary walking-stick with integral whisky flask (several styles available, from £40 to £300 depending on quality).

Davidoff

35 St James St., SW1 (B2)
☎ 020 7499 9950
⊖ Piccadilly Circus
Mon.-Fri. 9am-5.45pm, Sat.
9.30am-5.45pm.

Davidoff has the air and comforting odour of a gentleman's smoking room, where only the best cigars are smoked. Cuban cigars are their speciality, but all their accessories are in the best of taste.

Anything Left-handed

57 Brewer St., W1 (C2)
☎ 020 7437 3910
⊖ Leicester Square
Mon.-Sat. 9.30am-6pm.

The name of this little shop in Soho says it all: left-handed scissors, saucepans, fountain-pens and slide-rules. They also sell mugs and T-shirts with rallying calls or slogans demanding rights for the left-handed.

CARPETS AND RUGS IN SCOTTISH COLOURS

If you'd like to decorate your home in the style of a Scottish castle or English club, there's only one place to come for tartan furnishing fabrics and floorings: **Chatsworth Carpets**, 227 Brompton Rd, SW3, ⊖ Knightsbridge, ☎ 020 7584 1386. You won't find a great many designs on offer, but visitors from abroad can rest assured, none of them will be available back home. (Items delivered abroad.)

The Gadget Shop

Unit 8, Royal Opera House, Covent Garden Piazza., WC2 (C2)
☎020 7379 7922
⊖ Covent Garden
Mon.-Sat. 10am-8pm, Sun. noon-6pm.

Full of must-have gadgets and unusual gifts from the useful to the bizarre. The prices are very welcoming – you can buy a key ring for 50p, and what about that shocking pink, furry lamp?

Agent Provocateur

6 Broadwick St., W1 (C2)
⊖ Leicester Square
☎ 020 7439 0229
Mon.-Sat. 11am-7pm.

This lingerie shop opened by Joseph Corre, Vivienne Westwood's

son, has recently become the meeting-place for all the fashion writers, so get along there fast! Don't be put off by the window display – you can walk in with no worries, it isn't a sex shop. Inside you'll find very glamourous underwear with a 1950s feel, as well as more avant-garde designs.

Prowler of Soho

Brewer St., W1. (C2)
☎ 020 7734 4031
⊖ Leicester Square
Mon.-Thu. 11am-10pm,
Fri.-Sat. 11am-midnight,
Sun. noon-8pm.

This very busy shop is devoted to boys who love boys. The range of fashions on offer will enable you to find just the thing to make you stand out from the crowd in Heaven, as well as books, boys toys and, in a space on their own, videos. One of the hippest places in Soho. Girls are also welcome.

Spycatcher

25G Lowndes St., SW1 (B3)
☎ 020 7245 9445
⊖ Knightsbridge
Mon.-Fri. 9.30am-6pm,
Sat. 10am-5pm.

Budding James Bonds should make sure they pay a call here, where they'll find all the equipment a spy could wish for, from telephone bugging devices (illegal in some countries) to gadgets such as the world's most powerful whistle (this information hasn't been checked but you can always do that yourself if your ears aren't too sensitive).

Sherlock Holmes Memorabilia Company

230 Baker St., NW1 (off map)
☎ 020 7486 1426
⊖ Baker Street
Mon.-Fri. 9.30am-5.30pm,
Sun. 11am-4.30pm,
Sat. 10am-5pm.

Fans of Sir Arthur Conan Doyle's hero can buy his image in every

form imaginable on mugs or soft toys, and there's a great game where you live out his adventures.

Equinox – The Astrology Shop

78 Neal St., WC2 (C2)
☎ 020 7497 1001
⊖ Covent Garden
Mon.-Sat. 9am-7pm, Thu. 9am-8pm, Sun. 11am-7pm.

If the science of celestial influences is your thing, take a look in this little shop of a rather cosmic persuasion. You'll find luminous globes and moons for less than £2.

Mama Garr

Unit 49, Camden Lock Place (off map)
☎ 020 7284 0022
⊖ Camden Town

The only shop in London devoted to condoms. They come in all kinds of colours and flavours, from your everyday lemon and raspberry to intoxicating whisky or beer and exotic curry.

Penfriend

Bush House, Strand, WC2 (C2)
☎ 020 7836 9809
⊖ Temple
Mon.-Fri. 9.30am-5.30pm
34 Burlington Arcade
⊖ Piccadilly Circus
Mon.-Fri. 9.30am-5.30pm,
Sat. 10am-6pm.

This shop, a fountain-pen paradise, stocks all the major brands and everyone will find the new or second-hand pen that best suits their hand and purse. The shop can also repair any type of fountain-pen, or adapt them for left-handed writers.

Nightlife Practicalities

London is a paradise for late-nighters – in the centre of town you'll find people on the streets until two or three in the morning, and until dawn in Soho. Even in the depths of winter the pavements outside the clubs are always crowded with girls dressed only in short T-shirts or strappy dresses so they don't have to pay for the cloakroom. The advent of Eurostar has meant there's a weekend invasion from across the Channel just for a Saturday night in London. So, even if you're not the world's greatest techno fan, take a chance and experience something you may never find at home.

PUBS AND CAFÉS

If you don't have the stamina for dancing the night away after spending all day tramping round the city, there are lots of other things to do. Pubs, (Mon.-Sat. 11am-11pm, Sun. 11am-10.30pm), are always lively, particularly on Fridays, when Londoners let their hair down at the end of the week's work.

If you're visiting from abroad, here are some tips on what to expect from your visit to a pub. Pubs still have an important social role in Britain, and many workers round off their day in the pub. Many people have a regular pub, or 'local', near home or work. But there are so many good ones in London people, especially the young, energetic city-dwellers, often

DRESS CODE

With a few exceptions, most clubs do not pick and choose who to let in on the door. A few very smart places aside, you don't need to dress up and indeed your long dress or dark tie would be seen as inappropriate as fancy dress. At worst, they might even prevent you being let in. Eccentricity and dance gear are much appreciated in the hippest places, but they aren't the rule and if you go simply dressed everyone will think you've spent hours creating a 'non-look'.

have a selection they visit in different parts of town. Some pubs have big screens, and supporters of football or rugby will congregate to cheer on their teams when there's an important match on TV. In the centre, too, there's a new range of Irish pubs, and others where they serve traditional ales, bitters and the like, brewed by the small breweries.

The atmosphere in pubs is generally warm, noisy and smoky. The patrons talk, often very loudly, about local matters, events in the news or last night's match, and sometimes people play darts.

Pub and bar opening hours are changing all the time. In pubs that observe times strictly, there's still a rush to the bar to get in a last round when the 'last orders' bell is rung at 10.50 pm to remind customers that the pub will soon be closing. Pubs sell beer, cider and spirits, and the

choice of wines is improving. London also has some very good wine bars and brasseries, and there's a rash of new bars and drinking places. These are often themed and serve drinks and cocktails from other countries in the appropriate decor. Many of them have live music and performances at weekends. The trendiest bars are in the central areas of Soho, Piccadilly and Covent Garden. These are very busy in the evening.

CLUBS

The clubs open early, often around 10 pm, and are already full an hour later. It's cheaper to get in if you go before 11 pm. If you're lucky enough to have a student card, make sure you take it with you as it will often get you a reduction on the door. Most clubs and discos close at 3am, though some stay open until dawn.

Every week in London there are over two hundred different kinds of dance nights in the clubs and it can be difficult to find your way through the jungle to the one that's right for you. The principle is simple: each club provides a space that's run by different organisers every night. So your choice of club is based not on the place itself, but on the type of music it's hosting on any particular night.

What makes London's club scene so vital and varied is that the different nights change and develop very quickly. Your best bet is to phone first to check, or to

consult *Time Out* magazine, which provides details of what's on in each club, the type of music, the kind of crowd and so on.

SHOWS

If you want to book tickets for the theatre or ballet, you can do this through the London Tourist Board or British Travel Centre (see p. 33), or directly from your hotel. You can also try your luck at the ticket booking kiosk in Leicester Square (see p. 41).

Alternatively you can apply directly to the box office of the theatre or opera house that's staging the show you want to see. These are open from 10 am–8 pm. You'll find well-established private booking agencies throughout the city, but these take a 22% commission. Some agents are best avoided and you should be particularly wary of the ones you'll find in bureaux de change waiting to trap unsuspecting tourists. Don't expect to be able to get a seat in the stalls for the very popular shows and some are booked up months in advance. However, there are usually a few tickets available from the theatre box office on the night of the performance if you're prepared to queue outside the theatre two hours before the curtain rises. This is when any cancelled bookings are made available for re-sale.

PUBS

Bloomsbury

Finnegan's Wake

63 Lamb's Conduit St., WC1
☎ 020 7405 8278
⊖ Russell Square (C1)

This pub has the finest selection of English beers you'll find in London, but to appreciate them you'll have to bear with its very dark and smoky atmosphere. Not very relaxing or cosy, but ideal for connoisseurs who'd like to sample a rare ale.

Covent Garden

The Lamb and Flag

33 Rose St., WC2 (C2)
☎ 020 7497 9504
⊖ Covent Garden

This old, wooden building dates from 1623 and is one of the few buildings to have survived the Great Fire of London in 1666. Charles Dickens was a regular drinker here and it was formerly a venue for bare-knuckle boxing matches. A pleasant, traditional pub, full of history.

Holborn

Ye Olde Cheshire Cheese

145 Fleet St., EC4 (C2)
☎ 020 7353 6170
⊖ Blackfriars

In its 700-year history this pub has survived the Great Fire of London in 1666 (though it did have to be rebuilt afterwards), the German bombs of the Blitz in World War II and even the more recent mass migration of journalists out of the area. It's a real piece of history, with sawdust on the floor and dark little staircases. In the evening it's always full of tourists.

Princess Louise

208 High Holborn, WC1 (C2)
☎ 020 7405 8816
⊖ Holborn

The interior is listed, including the Victorian toilets, and you'll love drinking your beer surrounded by its decorated pillars and mirror fragments. The ground floor is dark and noisy with a great many animated conversations, but there's a quieter bar upstairs, where you won't have the latest headlines in *The Guardian* or the *Sun* bellowed in your ear to interrupt your pint.

Newman Arms

23 Rathbone St., W1 (C2)
☎ 020 7636 1127
⊖ Tottenham Court Road

A tiny pub, with a lively crowd, though they do have a few quieter tables outside. If you're not familiar with pubs, don't be put off if you have to drink standing up – that's the way it's done.

Soho

The French House

49 Dean St., W1 (C2)
☎ 020 7437 2799
⊖ Leicester Square

This was the second London headquarters of the exiled Free French led by General de Gaulle during the Second World War. The crowds spill out of the doors and onto the pavement. You can buy wine here and the place has a very relaxed atmosphere. A favourite haunt of many artists, writers and other Bohemian types and, of course, the French in exile.

Three Greyhounds

25 Greek St., W1 (C2)
☎ 020 7287 0754
⊖ Leicester Square

This pub, with its fine half-timbered façade, has a wide selection of beers on offer as well as simple but very good food to go with it. It's a great place to launch your crawl round the trendy bars of Soho, or to stop for a drink before going on to see a show at one of the many theatres on Shaftesbury Avenue.

Knightsbridge

Nag's Head

53 Kinnerton St., SW1 (B2)
☎ 020 7235 1135
⊖ Hyde Park Corner

The atmosphere here is calm and quiet, reminiscent of a country pub. You'd never believe you were in the centre of London. This impression is reinforced by the decor, which also tends towards the rustic, with its hunting scenes and bagpipes. However, if the weather's fine you can always drink your beer outside.

Charing Cross

Sherlock Holmes

10 Northumberland St., W1 (C2)
☎ 020 7930 2644
⊖ Charing Cross

Beers aside, this pub has the added draw of its collection of souvenirs connected with the great detective and the reconstructed study of his creator, Sir Arthur Conan Doyle. Conan Doyle used to drink here and even mentions the pub, under its former name of The Northumberland Arms, in his story 'The Hound of the Baskervilles'. Popular with tourists.

Orange Brewery

37 Pimlico Rd, SW1 (B3)
☎ **020 7730 5984**
⊖ **Sloane Square**

Here you can watch three local beers, amusingly named SW1, SW2 and Pimlico, fermenting away on the other side of a window. Of course you can also sample them (£1.85 for a pint) – in which case you'll discover just how excellent they are. One of the best pubs in London.

Enterprise

35 Walton St., SW3 (A3)
☎ **020 7584 3148**
⊖ **Knightsbridge**

The is *the* pub to choose if you feel rather intimidated at the thought of being surrounded by a huge crowd of people drinking beer and talking nineteen-to-the-dozen, which is what gives British pubs their charm. Here the tipple of choice is more likely to be champagne, and t-shirts are less common than shirts and ties. Call it up-market.

Finsbury

The Eagle

159 Farringdon Rd, EC1 (C1)
⊖ **Farringdon**
☎ **020 7837 1353**

This pub is popular for its good and very affordable food (£8.50 on average) and its own brand of beer (Charles Wells Eagle Bitter, £2 a pint). It also sells wine by the glass and has a few tables outside.

O'Hanlons

8 Tysoe St., EC1 (D1)
☎ **020 7837 4112**
⊖ **Angel**

This friendly Irish pub, with its crowd of regulars, has an authentic atmosphere and very good homemade food which is worth putting yourself out for. More to the point, it serves a selection of beers brewed by O'Hanlons' traditional brewery in wooden kegs, notably an award-winning Dry Stout. And you could also try their Guinness, which is drawn and served with appropriate reverence.

CAFÉS AND WINE BARS

Piccadilly

Atlantic Bar

20 Glasshouse St., W1 (C1)
☎ 020 7734 4888
⊖ Piccadilly Circus
Mon.-Fri. noon-2.45am, Sat.
Bar noon-3am, Sun. 6-10pm.

A few years ago when it was the trendiest place in town, you couldn't even set foot inside. It was heaving with media types. Now, it's a little easier to get in, but you should still make sure you dress up and don't bother making a fuss if they don't let you in, it won't make any difference. Inside it's stunning – a magnificent dance hall and smaller lounge in Art Deco style, plus a few famous faces. An ultra-swanky place to have a drink, particularly if you're out to impress.

Comedy Store

1 Oxendon St., SW1 (B2)
☎ 020 344 0234
⊖ Piccadilly Circus
Tue.-Fri. and Sun. 6.30-11pm, Fri.-Sat. 6.30pm-3am
Every day show 8-10.30pm,
Fri.-Sat. midnight-2.30am.

This establishment has been one of the most important venues staging stand-up comedy in London ever since the genre's great revival

nearly twenty years ago. You can come here to have dinner or, if you'd rather, just relax over a beer or two and let yourself be amused and entertained by quality performers in a buzzing atmosphere.

Café Royal

68 Regent St., W1 (B2)
☎ 020 7437 9090
⊖ Piccadilly Circus
Bar and restaurant
Mon.-Sat. 9am-11pm.

A great place to sample

delicious cocktails in peaceful surroundings. The rather high prices are justified by the quality and quantity of what you're served. There's no dress code, which is handy if you haven't remembered to pack your little black dress or smart suit.

Green Park

Che

23, St. James's St., SW1 (B2)
☎ 020 7747 9380
⊖ Green Park
Mon.-Sun. 11am-11pm.

This is an elegant bar in an elegant street that has recently been invaded by stylish, up-market restaurants and bars, often owned by city bankers. The interior here is sleek and Cool Britannia. You could just order a glass of wine but they specialise in a remarkable range of cocktails, served in chunky tumblers,

flavoured with exotic fruit juices and killer spirits. There's also a smoking room – the owner is passionately interested in cigars. The escalator in the entrance leads to a restaurant.

Covent Garden

Saint

8 Great Newport St., WC2 (C2)
☎ 020 7240 1551.
⊖ Leicester Square
Mon.-Thu. 5pm-3am,
Sat. 7.30pm-3am.

A trendy bar full of sharp young infotech entrepreneurs, gays and wannabe models. The management keeps very tight control on the door, so make sure you turn up looking hip. Expensive, but great music and the perfect place to show off.

Bar des Amis

11-14 Hanover Sq., WC2 (C2)
☎ 020 7379 3444
⊖ Covent Garden
Mon.-Sat. 11.30am-11.30pm.

As you'd expect from the name, you can drink French wines here, but there are also plenty from other countries if you prefer. If you're feeling peckish, try one of the cheese platters served with French bread.

Cork and Bottle

**44-46 Cranbourn St.,
WC2 (C2)
☎ 020 7734 6592
⊖ Leicester Square
Mon.-Sat. 11am-11.30pm.
Sun. noon-10pm.**

This is one of London's best wine bars. Its quiet little alcoves offer ideal spots to relax with a glass of wine and recover from the strain of shopping If you don't know what to try, the staff will give you excellent advice.

Freuds

**198 Shaftesbury Av., WC2 (C2)
☎ 020 7734 6592
⊖ Covent Garden
Mon.-Sat. 11am-11pm,
Sun. 11am-10.30pm.**

Anyone who feels nostalgic for the heady 1980s days of yuppies will feel right at home in this bar with its very sober decor of bare cement and metal. Others will appreciate the calm of its atmosphere and the unhysterical trendiness of its clientele of students and arty types. Live jazz on Sunday nights 8-10pm.

The Spot

**29 Maiden Lane, WC2 (C2)
☎ 020 7379 5900
⊖ Covent Garden
Mon.-Thu. noon-midnight,
Fri.-Sat. noon-1am,
Sun. noon-11pm.**

A great place to spend a pleasant evening in a relaxed atmosphere with jazz and soul sounds. At weekends you can watch the excitement mount until it's time for the crowds to leave

for the clubs, whether or not you choose to follow them. Comedy shows on Mondays.

Soho

Bar Italia

**22 Frith St., W1 (C2)
☎ 020 7437 4520
⊖ Tottenham Court Road**

Go to this bar when you've just left a club, around two or three in the morning. Being the only café that stays open round the clock, it's the meeting place for many of London's party animals. The patrons may be tired, but they keep on chatting and smiling just the same, spilling out onto the street clutching their cappuccinos. This is real Londoners' London, where you can strike up a conversation with anyone about anything to the sounds of kitsch Italian music. A must for atmosphere.

The Edge

11 Soho Square, W1 (B2)
☎ 020 7439 1313
⊖ Tottenham Court Road
Mon.-Sat. noon-1am,
Sun. 1-10.30pm.

Good-looking young men eye each
other from the corners of the four
floors of this originally 'men only',
though increasingly mixed bar, which
is a favourite with London's gays. But
the cruising stays fairly low-key and
the atmosphere is very friendly and
relaxed. Quiet during the day, with
tables outside on the square in
summer, busy in the evenings.

Freedom Café

60-66 Wardour St., W1 (C2)
☎ 020 7734 0071.
⊖ Leicester Square
Mon.-Sat. 11am-3am,
Sun. noon-1am.

One of the hippest places in town.
The ground floor bar is very popular
and you often have to queue to get
in. The basement has a room with a
stage, which regularly hosts gigs by
bands and other performers. A young,
trendy, mixed crowd.

100 Club

100 Oxford St., W1 (C2)
☎ 020 7636 0933
⊖ Tottenham Court Road
Mon.-Wed. 7.30pm-midnight,
Thu. 8pm-1am, Fri. 8.30pm-
2am, Sat. 7.30pm-2am, Sun.
7.30-11.30pm.

A great place for traditional jazz,
particularly on Friday nights, as the

beer pumps through the bloodstream
of both band and audience alike.
It's been a long time since the Sex
Pistols launched themselves onto an
unsuspecting world here.

Bloomsbury

The Old Crown

33 New Oxford St., WC1 (C2)
☎ 020 7836 9121
⊖ Tottenham Court Road
Mon.-Sat. noon-11pm.

Come here when the crowds of office-
workers have gone home after their
post-work bevvy and you'll find a
comfortable pub with pleasant
music, just the place for a quiet
drink.

Beach Blanket Babylon

45 Ledbury Rd, W11
(off map)
☎ 020 7229 2907
⊖ Notting Hill Gate
Mon.-Sat. noon-11pm,
Sun. 7-10.30pm.

Visit this place for the decor: an eclec-
tic-but-smart collection of bric-a-
brac, plus neo-Classical columns and
an awesome fireplace like the Gates
of Hell. A mixed crowd, but tending
towards the Yuppy. Lively, generally
good atmosphere.

CLASSIC DISCOS

Limelight

136 Shaftesbury Av., W1 (C2)
☎ 020 7434 0572

⊖ Leicester Square
Sun.-Thu. 7pm-1am,
Fri.-Sat. 2pm-2am.

A touch blasphemous? Dance the
night away in this former church
which has been converted into a club.
Mainly funk, garage and house
music, with a mixed crowd.

The Hippodrome

Cranbourne St., WC2 (C2)
☎ 020 7437 4311
⊖ Leicester Square
Mon.-Thu. and Sun. 9pm-
3am. Fri.-Sat. 9pm-3.30am.

With its giant neon horseman over
the door, this is one place you can't
fail to spot. Great sound system and
light show, a fairly conventional, well-
dressed crowd (no jeans here), trendy
girls and dance music.

Emporium

62 Kingly St., W1 (B2)
☎ 020 7734 3190
⊖ Oxford Circus
Mon.-Thu. 10pm-3am,
Fri.-Sat. 10am-4pm.

This well-behaved club boasts a few
celebrities and some charming young
West End ladies with their
dancing partners. The music is all
dance and the decor is like something
out of an Ibiza club, but it's not crazy
enough to blow you away.

Bar Rumba

36 Shaftesbury Av., W1 (BC2)
☎ 020 7287 2715
⊖ Piccadilly Circus
Mon.-Fri. 10-3.30am,
Sat. 7pm-6am.

To the sounds of acid jazz, salsa and
house, you can mingle with a crowd
of cool and trendy clubbers, who
arrive very early and bring the
atmosphere along awith them. Great
for those who don't like late nights.

Jazz Café

5 Parkway, NW1
(off map)
☎ 020 7916 6060
⊖ Camden Town
Fri.- Sat. 11.30pm-2am

(disco), every day 7pm-midnight for live music.

In this slightly cold blue decor some excellent acts play to a public of thirty-and forty-somethings. Jazz, acid jazz and sometimes rap, for those moments of relaxation. Some of the best live music in the city is played here.

Annabel's

44 Berkeley Sq., W1 (B2)
☎ 020 7629 2350
⊖ Green Park

You may have heard of Annabel's, but there's little point in trying to get in. This very exclusive club only admits members and the waiting lists are very long indeed. It appeals to a more middle-aged international set. You can have better fun a lot more easily elsewhere.

TRENDY CLUBS

The Blue Note

1 Hoxton Sq., N1 (D1)
☎ 020 7729 8440
⊖ Old Street
Mon.-Thu. and Sun. 10pm-3am, Fri.-Sat. 10pm-5am.

One of the most talked-about clubs in London in recent times, particularly the Sunday Metalheadz nights. Drum 'n' bass, trip-hop and jungle – all high-quality sounds, and a very friendly atmosphere.

Heaven

Underneath the Arches, Villiers St., WC2 (C2)
☎ 020 7839 3863

⊖ Charing Cross
Mon.-Fri. 10.30pm-3am.

Magnificent. Three floors packed with clubbers reflect Heaven's continued success for over 20 years. Thursday nights are trance, also frequented by New-Agers and the barely-old-enough, while Saturday nights are gay – a very happy atmosphere with techno, house and, on the top floor, disco sounds. One of the city's best.

Ministry of Sound

103 Gaunt St., SE1
(not on map.)
☎ 020 7378 6528
⊖ Elephant & Castle

Fri. 11pm-7am, Sat. 11pm-9am Sun. morning .

It's a bit of a trek from the centre to the true home of London techno. Two dancefloors, a cinema, video games and a bar. No alcohol is sold on the premises. There's always a crowd at the door, so it's not easy to get in, and the lucky ones are chosen on a whim.

The Fridge

Town Hall Parade, Brixton Hill, SW2 (not on map)
☎ 020 7326 5100
⊖ Brixton
Mon.-Thu. 10pm-3am, Fri.-Sat. 10pm-6am.

There's an enormous balcony overlooking the dancefloor, with a smaller room on the mezzanine. Several bars and a very warm, friendly atmosphere. Tuesday and Saturday nights are gay, as is Love Muscle night at weekends. Great techno nights on Fridays.

The Complex

1-5 Parkfield St., Islington N1 (D1)
☎ 020 7288 1986
⊖ Angel
Mon. and Thu.-Sat. 10.30pm-4.30am.

Opened with a bang but lives on as a fizzle. Three vast dancefloors and magnificent decor. On Fridays, the club plays host to the Voyager nights organised by Universe, the people behind the once-yearly Tribal Gathering, one of the biggest and best techno festivals in Europe. Also major international DJs every week.

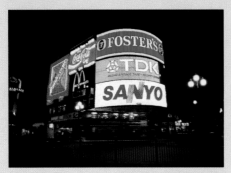

LONDON BY NIGHT

A walk through London on a warm summer's evening is a nice way to unwind after a busy day and it's generally pretty safe if you stick to the central parts full of people.

Starting from **Leicester Square**, you can walk down Gerrard Street into Chinatown which is usually very lively and buzzing with people. Its Chinese-style gates and telephone boxes make you feel as though you've been suddenly transported to Beijing.

Or you can start beneath the famous flashing signs of **Piccadilly Circus**, whose full effect can be properly appreciated only after dark. Either way, walk right into the heart of Soho, an area which is very busy all night long. Turn down Frith Street and stop off at the **Bar Italia** to revive yourself with a cappuccino in its warm and busy atmosphere.

Another pleasant walk takes you through the little streets of **Covent Garden**. Many of these have been pedestrianised, so you won't have to deal with much traffic. The area around the Piazza itself is usually full of people spilling out from pubs and cafés late into the night. Start off at the **Rock Garden** (The Piazza,

WC2 ☎ 020 7836 4052), a café that hosts live rock bands until 3am every night except Sundays. Then walk up James Street, past the tube station, cross over Long Acre and carry straight on, turning left into Earlham Street, in the centre of which you'll find **Seven Dials**. Take one of the roads to your right and you'll find yourself in Shaftesbury Avenue.

BUS TOURS
If you've been walking around all day you might like to treat yourself to a trip in a London bus at night to see the main sights illuminated. Only one company, **Golden Tours**, has departures right up to midnight

(☎ 020 7233 7030). If you take advantage of one of these tours you'll have the chance to explore London by night. **Evan Evans** (☎ 020 7950 1777) runs a *Bus Trip to Murder*, which takes you through the haunts of Jack the Ripper and Sweeney Todd. $3^{1}/_{2}$ hours of guaranteed shivers (£23 for adults, £21 for children).

RIVER TRIPS
The banks of the River Thames aren't as grand and elegant as those of some other cities and the sites are rather spread out along them, but there's a real sense of the link to the sea, particularly when low tide uncovers the beaches and the seagulls gather. A boat trip is a great way to explore the cityscape, with its bridges, warehouses and industrial buildings, many of which have been converted into flats, and the many different architechtural styles, including the massive dome of St Paul's Cathedral.

To take a boat trip down the Thames with dinner, the number to call is

☎ 020 7839 3572. If you don't want to have dinner on board, you can also take a trip to Greenwich. Last boats leave around 8.30pm.

Index

A

accommodation 68
AdHoc/Boy, kitsch clothes 88
Afro-Caribbean community 22
Agent Provocateur, shop 47–48, 113
airports 4–6
alcohol, duty free limits 7
Alfie's Antique Market 101
Angela Hale, jewellery 98
antiques, shops 100–101
Anything Left-Handed, shop 112
APC, clothes 87
Apple Market 105
Aquascutum, clothes 49, 82
Arena magazine, men's fashions 107
arts 13, 20–21
Asian community 22
Atlantic Bar 118
Austin Reed, men's fashions 91

B

banks, getting money 33
Barbour jackets, oilcloth 16
Baroque period 14–15
BBC Experience 21
Beauchamp Place, clothes 63
Bedford Square 53
beef, Scottish Aberdeen Angus 19
beer 19
Benjamin Pollock's Toy Shop 93
Berk, shopping 83
Berwick Street
   Market 104
   Soho 46
Big Ben 35
Bill Amberg, leather 89
black cabs 31
Black Out II, retro 44
Bloomsbury 52
   cafés/wine bars 120
   hotels 72
   pubs 116
   Wine Company 103
Bond International, clothes 88
Bond Street, hotels 70
Bond Street Antique Centre 57

Bone china 24
Box, The, bar 44
Brick Lane
   Indian restaurants 69
   Market 105
Britain Visitor Centre 9
British
   Airways 5
   cooking 69
   Midland 5
   Museum 52
Brixton Market 104
Brook's club 38
Brummell, Lord Beau 16
Buckingham Palace 11, 34
Buckle My Shoe, children's clothes 92
budgeting 8
Buffalo, shoes 43
Burberry, clothes 41
Bureaux de Change, commission 33
Burlington Arcade 37–38
   shopping 83
Burro, menswear 90
buses
   tours 9, 122
   travel 31
   trips 32
buying secondhand 109

C

Cadenhead's Covent Garden Whisky shop 103
Café Royal, cocktails 118
cafés 118–120
   practicalities 114–115
Camden Market 105
car hire 7
Carlton club 38
Carnaby Street 46–49
carpets/rugs, Scottish colours 113
Cenci, shop 44
Ceremony of the Keys 11
certificates of authenticity, art works 81
changing of the guard 11
Charing cross, pubs 116–117
charity shops 109
Chatsworth Carpets, tartan furnishings 113
cheeses 18–19, 103
Chelsea
   Flower Show 65
   King's Road 64–65

   pensioners 65
   restaurants 76
children's fashions 92–93
china, English 24–25, 49, 99
China Town 69
   Chinese New Year 22–23
Chinese restaurants 41, 69, 75
chintz, fabric 27
Christopher Wray, lamps 96
churches, Portland stone 15
Church's, shoes 57, 85
Chutney Mary, Indian restaurant 76
cigarettes, import limits 7
City airport 5
City, The, Square Mile 60–61
Claridge's
   hotel 70
   tea 59
clearance sales 85
Clone Zone, shop 51
clothes/accessories, shops 82–95
clubs 120–121
   gentlemen's 38
   practicalities 115
clubwear, clothes 87
coaches 4
cocktails 118
coffee 51
   houses 69
   shopping 102–103
Colefax and Fowler, chintz shop 27
Common Market, clothes 88
contemporary art 20–21
Contemporary Ceramics, shop 49
Cornucopia, dresses 109
Covent Garden 42–45
   cafés/wine bars 118–119
   hotels 73
   pubs 116
   restaurants 74
Crabtree & Evelyn, perfumes 111
Criterion Brasserie, restaurant 75
Crown Jewels, Tower of London 10, 61
cuisine, New British 18
cultural variety 22–23
currency 8
customs 7, 81

D

Daisy and Tom, toys 93
Davidoff, cigars 112
Deliss, shoes 89
department stores 94–95
Design museum 13
designer wear, women's
    fashions 86
disabled access, Liberty
    Drive 29
discount/secondhand
    shops, shopping
    106–109
Disney Store 47
Dispensary, clothes shop 48
Docklands 12
Downing Street 35
dress codes, clubs 115
Dr Marten's Store 43
Durrants Hotel 73
duty free shopping,
    European Union
    countries 81

E

Eagle, The, pub 117
East, clothes shop 86–87
Edward Lear Hotel 73
Elle magazine, fashions 107
embassies 6
emergency telephone
    number 8
Enterprise, pub 117
entry formalities, UK 7
Episode, clothes 87
*Equinox - The Astrology
    Shop* 113
Eskanazi, ivory 101
Eurostar, weekend 114

F

FA Premier League Hall
    of Fame 29
fabrics 26
fashion 12, 16–17
    magazines 107
Faxcessory, shop 111
Fielding Hotel 73
Finnegan's Wake, pub 116
Finsbury, pubs 117
fish 'n' chips 19
Fitzrovia, restaurants 77
food, import limits 7
Food for Thought, vegeta-
    rian restaurant 43–44
food/drink, shops 102–103
Forbidden Planet, comics
    110
Foreign Office 35
Formes, clothes shop 87
Fortnum & Mason's 37, 94
freight, delivery 81
Freud Museum 20

G

Gadget Shop 113
galleries 20–21
Gallery of Antique
    Costume and Textiles 101
gardens 28–29
Gatwick airport 5
gay London 50
Gerrard Street 41
getting there 4
Gieves and Hawkes,
    bespoke tailoring 91
gift shops 110–113
Go See, attraction pass 33
Gray's Antique Market 101
Great Fire of London
    14–15
Great Plague 14
Green Park
    cafés/wine bars 118
    restaurants 74
Greenhouse, restaurant 74
guided tours 9

H

haggling, markets 105
Hamleys, toy shop 47
Hampstead 66–67
    Heath 66
    hotels 72
    restaurants 76–77
handbags, shops 89
Harrods, shopping 63
Harvey Nichols 95
    fashion 63
hats 17
Hazlitt's, hotel 70
health 8
Heathrow airport 4
H.R. Higgins, teas 102
High Commissions 6
Holborn
    pubs 116
    restaurants 74
home decoration 96–97
hotels
    accommodation 70–73
    Bloomsbury 72
    Bond Street 70
    Covent Garden 73
    Hampstead 72
    Knightsbridge 71
    Marylebone 70
    Oxford Street 73
    Piccadilly 70
    practicalities 68–69
    Sloane Square 71
    Soho 70
    South Kensington 70–71
House of Cashmere,
    clothes 83
House of Commons 35
House of Lords 35

Humla Children's Shop
67, 92
Hyde Park 28
Hype DF, clothes 88

I

Ikkyu, Japanese restaurant
76
In-Wear, low prices 107
Indian Restaurants, Brick
    Lane 69
Institute of Contemporary
    Arts 35
insurance 7–8
internet cafés 33
Inventory, homeware shop
97
Irish community 23
Islington, restaurants 77
Italian community 23

J

Jamaica Wine House,
    coffee 61
James Hardy & Co,
    antiques 98
James Lock & Co, clothes
39
James Smith & Sons,
    umbrellas 53
Janet Fitch, giftshop 110
January Sales 85
Jermyn Street 17, 36–39
Jerry's Home Store,
    American homeware
97
Jess James, accessories 48
jewellery, shops 98
Jewish community 23
Jewish Museum 23
Jo Malone, beauty shop 86
John Gray, old luggage
    shop 111
John Lewis, shop 55, 95
John Lobb, shoes 39, 90
Jones, clothing 90
Jubilee Market 105

K

Karen Millen, clothes 87
Kensington
    Gardens 28
    Market 88
Kent and Curven, clothes
91
Kings of Sheffield,
    jewellery 98
Knightsbridge 62–63
    hotels 71
    pubs 116
Koh Samoui, clothes
44–45
Kokon to Zai, shop 51

L

La Gaffe, hotel 72
La Place, hotel 70
Lamb and Flag, pub 116
Landmark Hotel 70
Laura Ashley 46–47, 92
Leadenhall Market 104
Leicester Square 40–41
L'Homme Designer Exchange, menswear 109
Liberty, shop 47, 94
Liberty Drives, disabled access 29
Linen Merchant, shop 96
local time 9
Loft, The, clothes 44
London Eye 29
London Silver Vaults 98
London Transport Museum 42
London Underground, travel 30–31
London Zoo 29
Loong Fu supermarket, Chinese food 41
lost property 9, 31
Luton airport 5

M

MacKenzie's, shopping 36, 84
Madame Tussaud's 21
magazines, fashion 107
Mall, The 35
Mama Garr, condom shop 113
Manolo Blahnik, shoes 89
Mansion House, Lord Mayor of London 61
map, London 78–79
Map House, maps 101
Market, Covent Garden 42–43
markets, shopping 104–105
Marks and Spencer 54–55, 95
Marylebone, hotels 70
Mayfair 56–59
men's clothes sizes 91
men's fashions 90–91
Jermyn Street 17
Millennium Dome 13, 29
Milroy's Soho Wine Market, whiskies 51
minicabs 31
Ministry of Sound, clubs 12, 121
Mitsukoshi, Japanese restaurant 75
monuments, opening times 33
mosques 23
Muji, home accessories 47

multicultural London 22–23
Museum Store, reproductions 110
museums
British 52
Design 13
Freud 20
Jewish 23
London Transport 42
opening times 33
Victoria and Albert 23
music 21
muslim community 23

N

N Peal, cashmere 85
Nag's Head, pub 116
National Gallery 40
National Portrait Gallery 41
Neal's Yard Dairy, English cheese 45
Nelson's column, Trafalgar Square 40–41
New Mayflower, Chinese restaurant 75
nightlife 114–122
buses 31
Notting Hill carnival 22
Number Eleven, hotel 71

O

O'Hanlons, Irish pub 117
Oilily, children's clothes 93
Old Compton Street 50–51
opening times
museums 33
pubs 115
shops 80
Orange Brewery, pub 117
orchestras 21
organic food 19, 102
Oxfam Originals, charity shop 106
Oxford Street 54–55
hotels 73
restaurants 77

P

Palace Theatre, The 50
Palace of Westminster 35
Palomino, clothes 91
parks 28
Pâtisserie Valérie 51
Patrick Cox, shoes 89
Patrizia Wigan, children's clothes 93
Paxton & Whitfield, cheeses 103
paying, shops 80
Penfriend, pens 113
Penhaligon's, perfumes 61
personal shopping, clothes 95

pets 7
pharmacies 8
Photographer's Gallery 21
Physik Garden, Chelsea
Flower show 28–29
Piccadilly 36–39
cafés/wine bars 118
Circus 36, 75
hotels 70
Pied Bull Yard 53
piercing, body 13
Planet Organic, food 102
porcelain
English 24–25
maintenance 99
Portobello Road Market 105
opening times 80
Promenade concerts, Royal Albert Hall 21
Prowler of Soho, shop 113
pubs 116–117
football/rugby supporters 115
opening hours 115
practicalities 114–115

Q

quarantine 7

R

receipts, customs 81
Red or Dead, shoes 89
restaurants
Chelsea 76
Chinese 69
Covent Garden 74
Fitzrovia 77
Green Park 74
Hampstead 76–77
Holborn 74
Islington 77
Oxford Street 77
Piccadilly Circus 75
practicalities 69, 74–77
Soho 75
Strand 74
Rigby and Peller, designer wear 86
Ritz, The 38
river trips 9, 29, 32, 122
Rock circus 21
rooms, practicalities 68–69
Royal
Academy of Arts 37
Albert Hall 21
Doulton 39
Family 10–11
National Theatre 21
Opera House 42–43
Parks 28
Shakespeare Company 21

Royal Hospital, pensioners 65
Royal Worcester, china 25
R. Twining and Co, teas 103
Ruskin Hotel 72
Russell Square 53

S
St Christopher's Place, shops 55
St George's, Hanover Square 56
St George's Bloomsbury, church 53
St James's
church 36
Park 28, 35
St James's Street, exclusive clubs 56
Saint Martin-in-the-Fields, church 41
St Patrick's Day, Irish community 23
St Paul's cathedral 14, 15, 60
St Stephen's Walbrook 61
sales 5
Screen Face, shop 45
Selfridges, shop 55
Serpentine Lake 28
service charges, restaurants 69
Sherlock Holmes, pub 116–117
Sherlock Holmes Memorabilia Company 113
shoes 39
sizes 89
shopping
Bloomsbury 52–53
Carnaby Street 46–49
Chelsea 64–65
Covent Garden 42–45
Hampstead 66–67
Knightsbridge 62–63
Leicester Square 40–41
Mayfair 56–59
Old Compton Street 50–51
Oxford Street 54–55
Piccadilly Circus 36–39
practicalities 80–81
The City 60–61
shows, booking tickets 115
silver, shops 98
Simply Sausages, vegetarians 49
Simpson's in the Strand, restaurant 74
Sloane Square, hotels 71
Smallbone of Devizes, furniture 96
smoking 69
Smythson, stationery 57

Soho 46
cafés/wine bars 119
hotels 70
pubs 116
restaurants 75
Square 50
Sotheby's, auction house 56
South Kensington, hotels 70–71
Speaker's Corner, Hyde Park 54
Spitalfields Market, organic food 104
Spode, china 25
sportswear, clothes 87
Spycatcher, spy equipment 113
Stage & Screen, shop 110
Stansted airport 5
Stephen Jones, hats 83
Strand, restaurants 74
Streetwear, clothes 87
Sue Ryder, clothes 109
Swatch shop, Heathrow 81

T
tailors 16–17
tartans
The Scotch House 62
fabric 26–27
furnishing fabrics/floorings 113
taxis, travel 31
Taylor of Old Bond Street, personal grooming 39
tea 18, 51, 69, 102–103
Tea House, The 45
Techno, music 12
telephone accommodation booking service 68
telephone numbers, London 32
Thames, night trips 122
theatres 21
Thomas Burberry, clothes 82
Thomas Goode & Co, china/porcelain 99
Time Out magazine, clubs 115, 121
tipping 69
TK Maxx, designer labels 106
TM Lewin & Sons, shirts 90
Tops, fabrics 83
tourist information 9
tours
bus/boat 32
guided 9
Tower of London 11, 60
Trafalgar Square 40

trains 4
travel cards, costs 30
trench coats, style 16–17
Trotters, children's shop 93
Tube, travel 30–31
Turnbull and Asser, clothes 38
tweed, Harris 17

U
umbrellas 53

V
Vent, secondhand shop 109
Vexed Generation, clothes 48
Victoria and Albert Museum 23, 62
Vivienne Westwood 12
voltage 9

W
waiting times, made-to-measure 91
Wallace Collection, art 54
wallpaper, coating 97
Warner Bros Store 47
Waterford Wedgwood, china 38, 99
weapons, fines 7
Wedgwood, china 25, 38
Westaway and Westaway, clothes 53, 85
Westminster Abbey 34
what to see, practicalities 30–33
whiskies, shopping 103
Whistles, clothes shop 87
Whitehall, departments of State 35
Whittards, teas 102
William Shakespeare 21
wine bars 118–120
women's fashions 86–89
wool 27, 53
World's End Vivienne Westwood shop 65
Wren, Sir Christopher 14, 15

Y
Ye Olde Cheshire Cheese, pub 116
Yeoman 11
Yesterday's Bread, shop 108
Yo! Sushi, diner 48
Young England, children's clothes 92

Z
Zoo 29

Conversion tables for clothes shopping

Women's sizes

Shirts/dresses

U.K	U.S.A	EUROPE
8	6	36
10	8	38
12	10	40
14	12	42
16	14	44
18	16	46

Sweaters

U.K	U.S.A	EUROPE
8	6	44
10	8	46
12	10	48
14	12	50
16	14	52

Shoes

U.K	U.S.A	EUROPE
3	5	36
4	6	37
5	7	38
6	8	39
7	9	40
8	10	41

Men's sizes

Shirts

U.K	U.S.A	EUROPE
14	14	36
$14^{1}/_{2}$	$14^{1}/_{2}$	37
15	15	38
$15^{1}/_{2}$	$15^{1}/_{2}$	39
16	16	41
$16^{1}/_{2}$	$16^{1}/_{2}$	42
17	17	43
$17^{1}/_{2}$	$17^{1}/_{2}$	44
18	18	46

Suits

U.K	U.S.A	EUROPE
36	36	46
38	38	48
40	40	50
42	42	52
44	44	54
46	46	56

Shoes

U.K	U.S.A	EUROPE
6	8	39
7	9	40
8	10	41
9	10.5	42
10	11	43
11	12	44
12	13	45

More useful conversions

1 centimetre	0.39 inches	1 inch	2.54 centimetres
1 metre	1.09 yards	1 yard	0.91 metres
1 kilometre	0.62 miles	1 mile	1. 61 kilometres
1 litre	1.76 pints	1 pint	0.57 litres
1 gram	0.35 ounces	1 ounce	28.35 grams
1 kilogram	2.2 pounds	1 pound	0.45 kilograms

This guide was written by **Sarah de Haro** with **Catherine Laughton**
Translated by **Trista Selous** Updates and revises **Vanessa Dowell**
Project manager and copy-editor **Margaret Rocques**
Series editor **Liz Coghill**
Additional design assistance **Christine Bell**

We have done our best to ensure the accuracy of the information contained in this guide.
However, addresses, phone numbers, opening times etc. inevitably do change from time
to time, so if you find a discrepancy please do let us know. You can contact us at:
hachetteuk@orionbooks.co.uk or write to us at Hachette UK, address below.

Hachette UK guides provide independent advice. The authors and compilers do not accept any
remuneration for the inclusion of any addresses in these guides.

Please note that we cannot accept any responsibility for any loss, injury or inconvenience
sustained by anyone as a result of any information or advice contained in this guide.

Photo acknowledgements

Inside pages: **Christian Sarramon**: pp. 3 (r.c.), 10 (t.r.), 11(t.), 12 (t.r.), 17 (t.r.), 22 (b.r.), 26 (b.r.), 34, 35 (b.l., c.r.), 36, 37, 38 (b.c.), 39 (t.l., r. back and front, b.r.), 41 (t.l. and b.l.), 42 (c.r.), 43 (b.c.), 44 (c.), 45 (c.r, b.r.), 46 (b.l.), 47 (b.l., r., t.c.), 48 (t., b.r.), 49 (b.), 50 (b. back), 51 (b.l.), 53 (t.l.), 55 (b.), 56, 57 (b.l., t.c.), 58 (t.l.), 59 (b.), 61 (b.l.), 62 (t., b.r.), 63 (b.r.), 64, 65 (b.l. and c., t.r.), 66 (b.l.), 67 (t.c. c.r.), 82 (b.l. and r.), 94 (b.r.), 95 (t.r.), 101 (b.l., t.r.), 104, 105 (c.), 112 (b.r.), 113 (t.). **Robert Leslie**: pp. 3 (t.l, m.l.), 10 (b.), 11 (b.), 12 (b.), 13 (c.), 14 (b.l. and r), 15 (t.r.), 22 (t.l. and r., b.l.), 23, 35 (t.c.), 40 (b.r.), 41 (t.r.), 43 (b.l.), 44 (c.l. and r.), 45 (t.r.), 50 (b. front), 51 (t.r., b.r.), 53 (b.l., t.r.), 55 (t.l., c.r.), 60 (b.r.), 61 (b.r.), 63 (b.l. and c.), 67 (t.l., b.l. and r.), 74 (t.l., b.r.), 75, 76 (b.l., t.c.), 77, 93 (b. back), 95 (b. front), 100 (t.l. and r.), 101 (c.c., c.l.), 103 (t.r.), 107, 108 (b.c.), 116, 117, 118, 119, 120, 121, 122. **Sylvain Grandadam**: pp. 13 (t.r.), 20 (b.l.), 21 (t.l., b.c. and r.), 38 (t.l. and r., b.l.), 40 (b.l.), 51 (t.c.), 52, 60 (b.l.), 62 (b.l.), 65 (b.r.), 66 (b.r.), 74 (b.l.), 83 (t.r.), 85 (t.l.), 87 (t.l.), 93 (t.l.), 102 (b.r.), 106 (b.r.),108 (t r.) **Laurent Parrault**: p. 48 (b.l.), 51 (t.l.), 84 (c.l.), 88 (t.c.), 90 (c.), 102 (c., b.l), 109 (b.r. and t.r.) **Hachette Livre**: pp.12 (t.l.), 14 (t.), 15 (l. and b.), 16 (t.r.), 18 (c.t.), 20 (b.r., t.), 25 (t.c.), 98 (b. and c.).**G. Bouchet/*ELLE***: pp. 21 (t.r.), 59 (t.l.), 86 (b.l.), 89 (b.l.), 93 (t.l.), 94 (t.), 97 (t.l.), 103 (t.c. front), 105 (t.l. and r., b.), 111 (t.l.), **G. Pascal/*ELLE***: pp. 16 (b.l., t.l.), 18 (c.c.c.), 24 (t.l. and r.), 25 (c.l. and r.c.), 27 (t.c., b.r.), 41 (b.r.), 57 (t.r.), 83 (t.c.), 90 (t. and c.), 103 (b.l. and t.c. back), 111 (b.l. and c.r.).**Éric Guillot**: pp. 106 (t.c.), 109 (b.l., b.c.), 112 (c.r.), 113 (b.r.).**The Sun**: p. 10 (t.l.) **I-D.**: p. 12 (t.l.). **Church's**: pp. 17 (b.l.), 57 (b.r.), 85 (b.). **Dr Martens**: pp. 17 (b.c.), 43 (t.l.), 84 (t.l.). **Duffer**: pp. 17 (b.r.), 91 (t.l.). **I. Rozenbaum/F. Cirou, Photo Alto**: pp. 18 (b. and t. l. back), 19 (b.c.). **Royal Doulton**: pp. 24 (b.), 25 (b.), 99. **Sanderson**: pp. 26 (b.l.), 100 (b). **N Peal**: pp. 27 (t.r.). **J. Lobb**: p. 39 (b.l.). **Tea House**: p. 45 (t.l.). **Screen Face**: p. 45 (b.l.) **Liberty textiles**: pp. 46 (b.r.), 94 (b.c.). **Muji**: pp. 47 (c. front and back). **Contemporary Ceramics**: p. 49 (t.). **James Smith & Sons**: pp. 53 (b.r.), 112 (t .front and back, c.l.). **Peter Tebbit**: p. 54. **DKNY**: pp. 58 (t.r. front and back). **Swaine**: p. 82 (t., c.r.). **Jigsaw**: p. 58 (c., c.r.). **Claridges**: p. 59 (t.r.). **Penhaligon's**: pp. 61 (b.c.), 111 (b.c .and r.). **Steinberg & Tolkien**: pp. 64 (t.l.). **Coast**: p. 74 (t.r.). **Chutney Mary**: p. 76 (b.r.). **Stephen Jones**: p. 83 (c.l.). **Mulbery**: p. 84 (b.r.). **Caroline Charles**: p. 86 (t.r.). **Voyage**: p. 86 (c.). **Formes**: p. 87 (b.c.). **Bill Amberg**: p. 89 (c.l., b.l.). **Deliss**: p. 89 (b. and t. r.). **TM Lewin & Sons**: p. 90 (b.c.). **Austin Reed**: p. 91 (b.c.). **Gieves & Hawkes**: p. 91 (t.r.). **Kent & Curven**: p. 91 (b.l.). **Young England**: p. 92 (b.r.). **Buckle my Shoe**: p. 92 (b.l.). **Benjamin Pollock's toy Shop**: p. 93 (c.c.). **George Rech**: p. 95 (b.r.). **Smallbone of Devizes**: p. 96. **Laura Ashley**: p. 97 (c.l.). **Rj's Homeshop**: p. 97 (t.r; b.c.). **Peter Jones**: p. 98 (t.l.). **Gallery of Antique costumes and textiles**: p. 101 (b.r.) **Janet Fitch**: p. 110 (b.l.); **Space NK**: p.110 (c.). **Martin Jones**: p. 28 (b.l., t.r.) **Rob Moore**: p. 42 (c.b.) **Derek Harris**: p. 29 (t.l.) **Jeremy Young/GMJ**: p. 20 (t.l.)

Front cover: **Ch. Sarramon**: t l.; c.c. ; c.r. ; b.l. **R. Bokelberg, Image Bank**: t.c **R. Leslie**: t.r.; b.r. **Ch.Bissell**, **Fotogram Stone**: b.c. front. **Janet Gill, Fotogram Stone**: c.l. **J.-P. Fruchet**, **Pix**: c.r. front
Back cover: **Ch. Sarramon**: t.r.; c.l. **R. Leslie**: b.l. **Royal Doulton**: c. front.

Illustrations: Pascal Garnier.
Cartography © Hachette Tourisme/London Underground map © *London Transport Museum*

First published in the United Kingdom in 2000 by Hachette UK

© English Translation, completely revised and updated, Hachette UK 2000
© Hachette Livre (Hachette Tourisme) 1998

Distributed in the United States of America by Sterling Publishing Co., Inc.
387 Park Avenue South, New York, NY 10016-8810

A CIP catalogue for this book is available from the British Library

ISBN 1 84202 013 7

Hachette UK, Cassell & Co., The Orion Publishing Group, Wellington House, 125 Strand,
London WC2R 0BB

Printed and bound in Italy by Milanostampa S.P.A.

If you're staying on for a few days and would like to try some new places, the next pages give you a wide choice of hotels, restaurants and bars, listed by district and with addresses.

Although you can just turn up at a restaurant and have a meal (except in the most prestigious establishments), don't forget to book your hotel several days in advance (see page 68).

Enjoy your stay!

STAYING ON A LITTLE LONGER

The hotels on the following list are classified by district. The prices quoted are indicative only and are for a double room with en-suite bathroom or shower. Generally speaking, prices do not include breakfast.

Victoria/Westminster

Brindle House Hotel
1 Warwick Place North
SW1V 1QW
⊖ Victoria
☎ 020 7828 0057
🖷 020 7931 8805
£45
Good value for money in this small hotel with an excellent location. An ideal place to relax after a long day's sightseeing.

Elizabeth Hotel
37 Eccleston Square
SW1V 1PB
⊖ Victoria
☎ 020 7828 6812
From £55 to £85
Located in one of the smart districts of London a few minutes from Buckingham Palace, this hotel's prices are surprisingly affordable. You'll also have access to the private gardens and tennis courts of the residents of Eccleston Square.

Luna-Simone Hotel
47 Belgrave Rd
SW1V 2BB
⊖ Victoria
☎ 020 7834 5897
🖷 020 7828 2474
From £35 to £55
You'll get a warm welcome at this hotel a few minutes from the tube, rail and bus stations at Victoria. Very handy for getting to the city's main centres.

Melita House Hotel
35 Charlwood St.
SW1V 2DU
⊖ Pimlico
☎ 020 7834 1387
🖷 020 7932 0988
From £40 to £55
A small family-run hotel where you'll be made to feel completely at home. Very near the tube.

Woodville House Hotel
107 Ebury St.
SW1W 9QU
⊖ Sloane Square
☎ 020 7730 1048
£45
Not very large or luxurious, this hotel in a Georgian building is ideal for tourists on a limited budget. You can also enjoy the garden in summer.

Windermere Hotel
142-144 Warwick Way
SW1V 4JE
⊖ Victoria
☎ 020 7834 5840
🖷 020 7630 8831
From £50 to £80
The first thing you notice is the magnificent Victorian façade. The interior is pleasant and modern.

Around Marble Arch

Concorde
50 Great Cumberland Pl.
W1H 7FD
⊖ Marble Arch
☎ 020 7402 6316
£85
Simple and welcoming, a hotel located near Oxford Street.

The Edward Lear Hotel
30 Seymour St.
W1H 5WD
⊖ Marble Arch
☎ 020 7402 5401
🖷 020 7706 3766
From £55 to £85
Located in the heart of London, very near Oxford Street, this is a simple, pleasant hotel and the rooms are modern and comfortable.

Lincoln House Hotel
33 Gloucester Pl.
W1H 3PD
⊖ Baker Street
☎ 020 7486 7630
🖷 020 7486 0166
From £60 to £90
A Georgian-style hotel with a superb location. The prices are reasonable for the area and the quality of service.

Marble Arch Inn
49-50 Upper Berkeley St.
W1H 7PN
⊖ Marble Arch
☎ 020 7723 6060
From £75 to £89
A few minutes from Hyde Park and Oxford Street, you can see everything from here.

Paddington/Bayswater

Abbey Court Hotel
174 Sussex Gardens
W2 1TP
⊖ Paddington
☎ 020 7792 0858
🖷 020 7262 2055
From £40 to £55
All the rooms in this luxury hotel are decorated in a Victorian style. You will be only a few minutes away from Notting Hill Gate as well as the famous and particularly lively Portobello Road Market.

Byron Hotel
36-38 Queensborough Terrace
W2 3SH
⊖ Bayswater
☎ 020 7243 0987
🖷 020 7792 1957
From £50 to £90
You'll receive a warm welcome at this simple, modest hotel near the magnificent Kensington Gardens.

Duke of Leinster
34 Queen's Garden
W2 3AA
⊖ Bayswater
☎ 020 7258 0079
🖷 020 7262 0741
From £69 to £74
Near Hyde Park and only minutes from Queensway.

Dylan Hotel
14 Devonshire Terrace
W2 3DW
⊖ Bayswater
☎ 020 7723 3280
🖷 020 7402 2443
From £40 to £55
Facing Hyde Park and a few minutes from Oxford Street in one direction and Notting Hill Gate on the other. Very reasonable prices.

Hyde Park Rooms Hotel
137 Sussex Gardens
SW2 2RX
⊖ Paddington
☎ 020 7723 0965
From £38 to £50
This clean comfortable and welcoming hotel, is a few minutes walk from Hyde Park and the tube station at Paddington. A good hotel.

Prince William Hotel
42-44 Gloucester Terrace
W2 3DA
⊖ Royal Oak
☎ 020 7724 7414
🖷 020 7706 2411
From £45 to £75
*Very close to Paddington,
Bayswater and Hyde Park,
you'll have use of the lounge,
restaurant and bar.*

Royal Park Hotel
2-5 Westbourne Terrace
W2 3UL
⊖ Bayswater
☎ 020 7402 6187
🖷 020 7224 9426
From £78 to £80
*Built in 1851, this hotel has been
recently renovated. Comfortable
and welcoming.*

St. David's and Norfolk Court Hotel
16 Norfolk Square
W2 1RS
⊖ Paddington
☎ 020 7723 3856
🖷 020 7402 9061
From £45 to £55
*Looking on to a square, this is a
peaceful, welcoming hotel. It also
prides itself on providing the best
English Breakfast in London.*

SASS House Hotel
10-11 Craven Terrace
W2 3QD
⊖ Lancaster Gate
☎ 020 7262 1723
🖷 020 7262 1764
From £35 to £54
*Ideal for those on a limited
budget. A very good location
between the West End and
Notting Hill Gate.*

Parkwood Hotel
4 Stanhope Place
W2 2HB
⊖ Marble Arch
☎ 020 7402 2241
From £59 to £65
*Just a couple of minutes from
Oxford Street and the famous
Speaker's Corner in Hyde Park
and not far from Buckingham
Palace. Comfortable rooms.*

Thistle Kensington Gardens Hotel
9 Kensington Gardens
Square
W2 4BH
⊖ Royal Oak

☎ 020 7221 4560
🖷 020 7221 4560
From £70 to £75
*The building is both Victorian
and modern, near the Bayswater
district and Queensway.*

Chelsea/ Earl's Court/ South Kensington

Abcone Hotel
10 Ashburn Gardens
SW7 4DG
⊖ Gloucester Road
☎ 020 7370 3383
🖷 020 7373 3082
From £50 to £90
*Near the very fashionable area of
High Street Kensington and most
of the big museums (Victoria and
Albert Museum, Natural History
Museum, Science Museum).*

Lord Jim Hotel
23-25 Penywern Rd
SW5 9TT
⊖ Earls Court
☎ 020 7370 6071
🖷 020 7373 8919
From £30 to £50
*Very well located for visiting the
Natural History and Science
Museums. Close to Earls Court
tube station, which gives you
access to the West End in about
15 minutes.*

Merlyn Court Hotel
2 Barkston Gardens
SW5 0EN
⊖ Earls Court
☎ 020 7373 8285
🖷 020 7370 4986
*This family-run hotel overlooks
a green and pleasant square.
Well placed for Earls Court tube.*

Mowbray Court Hotel
28-32 Penywern Rd
SW5 9SU
⊖ Earls Court
☎ 020 7370 2316
🖷 020 7370 5693
From £55 to £60
*A luxury hotel with reasonable
prices, located near Earl's Court,
the exhibition centres and
museums.*

Rascool Court Hotel
19-21 Penywern Rd
SW5 9TT
⊖ Earls Court
☎ 020 7373 8900
🖷 020 7244 6835
From £40 to £46

In this street lined with hotels, the Rascool is one of the least expensive.

Windsor House
12 Penywern Rd
SW5 9ST
☉ Earls Court
☎ 020 7373 9087
🖷 020 7385 2417
From £34 to £50
Very well located for all amenities and close to the tube. An ideal hotel for those on limited budgets.

Amsterdam Hotel
7 Trebovir Rd
SW5 9LS
☉ Earls Court
☎ 020 7370 2814
🖷 020 244 7608
From £80 to £95
The prices are certainly a little high, but they are well justified. Comfortable, modern rooms and quality service.

York House Hotel
27-28 Philbeach
Gardens
SW5 9EA
☉ Earls Court
☎ 020 7373 7579
🖷 020 7370 4641
£47
Just a few minutes from the Earls Court exhibition centre, this hotel is very well served with transport.

Swiss House Hotel
171 Old Brompton Rd
SW5 0AN
☉ Earls Court
☎ 020 7373 2769
🖷 020 7373 4983
£75
This is a lovely hotel located near the museums and exhibition centres. Voted best Bed and Breakfast in London, so the prices are a little high. A place to remember.

Kensington/ Holland Park

Abbey House
11 Vicarage Gate
W8 4AG
☉ Notting Hill Gate
☎ 020 7727 2594
£65
This very quiet hotel is located near a square in a residential district.

Further afield

La Reserve
422-428 Fulham Rd
SW6 1DU
☉ Parsons Green
☎ 020 7385 8561
£99
This hotel boasts a classic exterior and very unusual interior The decor is ultra-modern and the rooms are decorated in minimalist style. Perfect for those who want to stay in trendy surroundings.

Swiss Cottage
4 Adamson Rd
NW3 3HP
☉ Swiss Cottage
☎ 020 7722 2281
£100
Very near the tube and a few minutes bus ride from Hampstead Village, this Victorian building in classic style has an interesting collection of paintings. The rooms are very large and comfortable and the most expensive have velvet-covered sofas and chaises-longues.

HOTELS

The following list provides a selection of restaurants, serving food from Britain and around the world. Greek, Japanese or Turkish cuisine like you've never tasted before.

Chelsea

AMERICAN

Big Easy
332-334 King's Rd, SW3
⊖ Fulham Broadway
☎ 020 7352 4071
Bring the whole family to this fun restaurant with a young feel. The portions are huge, the music's loud and a good atmosphere is guaranteed.

Cactus Blue
86 Fulham Rd, SW3
⊖ Fulham Broadway
☎ 020 7823 7858.
Funky atmosphere and unusual food in modern surroundings

BRITISH

Foxtrot Oscar
79 Royal Hospital Rd, SW3
⊖ Sloane Square
☎ 020 7352 7179
More of a bistrot than a restaurant where you can sample Anglo-American specialities. Good value for money.

SPANISH

El Blason
8-9 Blacklands Terrace, SW3
⊖ Sloane Square
☎ 020 7823 7383
Subtle Spanish cuisine with a tapas bar in the basement.

THAI

Thai on the River
Chelsea Wharf,
15 Lots Rd, SW10
⊖ Fulham Broadway
☎ 020 7351 1151
As its name suggests, this Thai restaurant is on the banks of the river Thames. A very pleasant setting for this very smart establishment, however it can be rather expensive .

Chinatown

CHINESE

Golden Dragon
26 Gerrard St., W1
⊖ Leicester Square
☎ 020 7734 2763.
One of the best Chinese restaurants in Chinatown although it's very noisy. Go early to avoid the queues.

New World
1 Gerrard Place, W1
⊖ Leicester Square
☎ 020 7734 0396.
Good value for money in this resturant, where you can sample cuisine from all the different regions of China. Truly excellent dim-sum.

JAPANESE

Tokyo Diner
2 Newport Place, WC2
⊖ Piccadilly Circus
☎ 020 7777 6999
Simple and affordable. Ideal for a quick meal before you go out.

City

AMERICAN

Arkansas Café
Unit 12, Old Spitalfields Market, E1
⊖ Liverpool Street
☎ 020 7377 6999
This bistrot prides itself on serving the best American-style steak in London. Judge for yourself!

BRITISH

City Rhodes
1 New Street Square, EC4
⊖ Holborn
☎ 020 7583 1313
This restaurant is hard to find, but don't give up! It's well worth making the effort! Here you can sample modern British cuisine.

Clapham

GREEK

Sappho Meze Bar
9 Clapham High St., SW4
⊖ Clapham North
☎ 020 7498 9009
Generous portions of simple food in a warm and lively atmosphere.

THAI

Pepper Tree
198 Clapham Common Southside, SW4
⊖ Clapham Common
☎ 020 7622 1758.
Good food at reasonable prices in this little restaurant that looks like a cafeteria. A lovely place to have dinner with friends rather than a romantic evening for two.

Covent Garden

AFRICAN

Calabash
The Africa Centre
38 King St., WC2
⊖ Covent Garden
☎ 020 7836 1976
Exciting cuisine from countries from all over the entire continent of Africa, all at affordable prices. In the evenings, there are live performances in the club.

Souk
2 Litchfield St., WC2
⊖ Leicester Square
☎ 020 7240 1796
It can be hard to find this East African restaurant at first (it's tucked away next door to The Ivy), but once you do, you will find a Moroccan grotto complete with candles, comfy sofas and plenty of atmosphere. The waiters will occasionally sing, dance and bang their drums. Good, filling food which is quite simple but very tasty and moderately priced.

AMERICAN

Maxwell's
8-9 James St., WC2
⊖ Covent Garden
☎ 020 7836 0303
Very American cuisine and atmosphere in this restaurant which is packed out at weekends. It's best to go early.

PJ's Grill
30 Wellington St., WC2
⊖ Covent Garden
☎ 020 7240 7529
This place is famous for its cocktails. Lively, wine bar atmosphere.

BRITISH

Porters Restaurant
16-17 Henrietta St.,
WC2
⛵ Covent Garden
☎ 020 7836 6466
www.porters.uk.com
Lovely grub! Sausages and mash, liver and onions – traditional British cooking in an ideal location for a pre-theatre meal.

MEXICAN

Café Pacifico
5 Langley St., WC2
⛵ Covent Garden
☎ 020 7379 7728
Lively Mexican bar and restaurant in Covent Garden offering a wide range of moderately priced dishes with an extensive drinks list. Eating isn't compulsory but beware – running up a tab at the bar can be unexpectedly expensive as the margaritas are very drinkable…

Greenwich

CHINESE

**Tai Wan Mein
(Noodle House)**
49 Greenwich Church St.
SE10
Train: Greenwich
☎ 020 8858 1668
A simple menu of authentic chinese cuisine, served quickly.

Hampstead

JAPANESE

Jinkichi
73 Heath St., NW3
⛵ Hampstead
☎ 020 7794 6158
A small Japanese restaurant specialising in grills.

Knightsbridge

GOOD VALUE

Stockpot
6 Basil St., SW3
⛵ Hyde Park Corner
☎ 020 7589 8627
Basic, but filling food. Ideal for those on limited budgets. Try the bargain set lunches.

CHINESE

Mr Chow
151 Knightsbridge, SW1
⛵ Knightsbridge
☎ 020 7589 7347
Excellent cuisine and impeccable service. This chinese restaurant has two other branches, one in New York and the other in Beverly Hills.

ITALIAN

Zafferano
15 Lowndes St., SW1
⛵ Sloane Square
☎ 020 7235 5800
Seasonal dishes from a very fine Italian kitchen served in an under-stated decor. Be sure to book a table for the brilliant set lunch.

Pizza on the Park
11 Knightsbridge, SW1
⛵ Knightsbridge
☎ 020 7235 5273
An elegant pizzeria overlooking Hyde Park. Jazz and cabaret in the evenings.

Marble Arch

INDIAN

Porte des Indes
3, Bryanston St., W1
⛵ Marble Arch
☎ 020 7224 0055
Excellent cuisine, luxurious interior, but expensive.

Marylebone

CHINESE

Royal China
40 Baker St., W1
⛵ Baker Street
☎ 020 7487 3123
Lots of seafood on the menu, but don't forget to try the excellent dim sum.

IRISH

Ard Ri Dining Room
88 Marylebone Lane, W1
⛵ Marble Arch
☎ 020 7935 9311
Located above the O'Conor Don pub, this restaurant serves traditional Irish fare with a modern edge. The set menu is excellent value.

RESTAURANTS

Mayfair

AMERICAN

Hard Rock Café
150 Old Park Lane, W1
🚇 Green Park
☎ 020 7629 0382
This chain of restaurants has spread all over the world and you come here more for the atmosphere and decor than for the food, which is nothing out of the ordinary.

BRITISH

Dorchester Grill Room
The Dorchester
54 Park Lane, W1
🚇 Marble Arch
☎ 020 7629 8888
If you want a romantic dinner for two, there's no two ways about it, you must come to the Dorchester. The smartest of the smart restaurants, it is located in the hotel of the same name.

Greenhouse
27A Hay's Mews, W1
🚇 Green Park
☎ 020 7499 3331
This restaurant has an established and entirely justified reputation. Perfect food and service.

CHINESE

Zen Central
20-22 Queen St., W1
🚇 Green Park
☎ 020 7629 8089
Don't be fooled by the modern interior, the cuisine is entirely traditional.

JAPANESE

Benihana
37 Sackville St., W1
🚇 Piccadilly Circus
☎ 020 7494 2525
Impressive restaurant where the chefs demonstrate their culinary skills before your very eyes.

Nobu
19 Old Park Lane, W1
🚇 Green Park
☎ 020 7447 4747.
One of the most highly regarded Japanese restaurants in London. Very smart and very expensive.

ITALIAN

Condotti
4 Mill St. W1
🚇 Piccadilly Cicus
☎ 020 7499 1308
Excellent pizzas with generous toppings in a mediterranean atmosphere.

TURKISH

Sofra
18 Shepherd St., W1
🚇 Green Park
☎ 020 7493 3320
Perfect for lunch, this restaurant serves snacks and hot meals, but beware, prices are rather high.

Notting Hill

ITALIAN

Calzone Pizza Bar
2A Kensington Pk Rd, W11
🚇 Ladbroke Grove
☎ 020 7243 2003
Tasty, generous pizzas and calzones. Good for a quick snack on the way back from Portobello Market.

THAI

Churchill Arms
119 Kensington Church St., W8
🚇 Notting Hill Gate
☎ 020 7727 4242
At first sight it looks like just another pub, but don't let that put you off. The restaurant is in the back room, behind the bar.

Paddington

FRENCH

Bistro Daniel
26 Sussex Place, W2
🚇 Paddington
☎ 020 7723 8395
Resolutely French cuisine in both the bistro and the smarter restaurant upstairs, with a few of Daniel's innovative, personal touches.

MALAYSIAN & INDONESIAN

Satay House
13 Sale Place, W2
🚇 Paddington
☎ 020 7723 6763

Authentic and inexpensive Malaysian and Indonesian dishes.

Piccadilly

AMERICAN

Gaucho Grill
19 Swallow St., W1
🚇 Piccadilly Circus
☎ 020 7734 4040
This restaurant's great speciality is 'steak that melts in your mouth'. An absolute must for carnivores.

Planet Hollywood
Trocadero
13 Coventry St., W1
🚇 Leicester Square
☎ 020 7287 1000
The restaurant chain owned by Hollywood stars. The food is perfectly fine if not very original. Cross your fingers, you might run into Bruce Willis!

JAPANESE

Yoshino
3 Piccadilly Place, W1
🚇 Piccadilly Circus
☎ 020 7287 6622
The menu changes every day depending on how the chef's feeling, but there's always a lot of fish dishes.

MEXICAN

Down Mexico Way
25 Swallow St., W1
🚇 Piccadilly Circus
☎ 020 7437 9895
For a vibrant, noisy and energetic evening!

Putney

BRITISH

Hudsons
Lower Richmond Rd, SW15
Train: Putney
☎ 020 8785 4522
This great little restaurant serves breakfast, lunch and dinner at a good price. The menu always presents problems as there are too many nice dishes to choose from!

Phoenix
Pentlow St., SW15
🚇 Putney Bridge, then bus 22 or 265 towards Barnes

☎ 020 8780 3131
The Phoenix Bar & Grill has food and service comparable to Conran restaurants like Bluebird, yet is about half the price. Well worth making the trip to SW15.

Soho

AMERICAN

Blues Bistro & Bar
42-43 Dean St., W1
⊖ Tottenham Court Rd
☎ 020 7494 1966
Lively bar with a very mixed crowd and a very Soho atmosphere.

Boardwalk
18 Greek St. W1
⊖ Tottenham Court Rd
☎ 020 7287 2051.
Classic American cuisine, reasonably priced. The most interesting things here are the cajun dishes, try the catfish or the crab cakes. Must be sampled.

BRITISH

Cafe Emm
17 Frith St., W1
⊖ Tottenham Court Rd
☎ 020 7437 0723
Great value, good food with large portions, served in an appealing intimate bistro-type atmosphere. Can get busy though, and you may have to queue for a table.

CHINESE

Ming
35-36 Greek St., W1
⊖ Tottenham Court Rd
☎ 020 7734 2721
You'll find a wide selection of delicious specialities in this simple, authentic-feeling restaurant.

INDIAN

Soho Spice
124-126 Wardour St., W1
⊖ Tottenham Court Rd
☎ 020 7434 0808
This restaurant is in one of the liveliest streets in Soho. There's a good atmosphere, particularly in the evening.

JAPANESE

Hi Sushi
40 Frith St., W1
⊖ Tottenham Court Rd
☎ 020 7734 9688
A sushi bar on the ground floor and low tables in the basement, where you eat your sushi etc. sitting on the floor, Japanese style.

Kulu Kulu
76 Brewer St., W1
⊖ Piccadilly Circus
☎ 020 7734 7316
Here you choose your dishes as they glide past you in a tempting line on a conveyor belt. This little restaurant has an established quite a reputation for itself and is often packed out.

St James

BRITISH

Wiltons
55 Jermyn St., SW1
⊖ Green Park
☎ 020 7629 9955
A British restaurant that specialises in fish and seafood dishes.

JAPANESE

Matsuri
15 Bury St., SW1
⊖ Green Park
☎ 020 7839 1101
Superb sushi and excellent teppanyak are served in this modern, welcoming Japanese restaurant.

Southwark

BRITISH

Fish!
Cathedral St.,
Borough Market, SE1
⊖ London Bridge
☎ 020 7836 3236
E-Mail:
info@fishdiner.co.uk
Web:
www.fishdiner.co.uk
Basic menu with the freshest, tastiest fish available at the time. The side orders feature the smoothest, creamiest mashed potato ever created by man.

RESTAURANTS

BRITISH

Butlers Wharf Chop House
Butlers Wharf Building
36E Shad Thames, SE1
⊖ Borough
☎ 020 7403 3403
This restaurant has a magnificent location on the 36th floor of the building, giving you an exceptional view over London as you eat your meal.

INDIAN

Bengal Clipper
11 Shad Thames
Butlers Wharf, SE1
⊖ Borough
☎ 020 7357 9001
From the nan bread, to the tandoori chicken or vindaloo, everything's good here, the only problem is deciding which dishes to choose.

GOOD VALUE

Café in the Crypt
Crypt of St Martin-in-the-Fields
Duncannon St., SE1
⊖ Covent Garden
☎ 020 7839 4342
An unusual setting in a central location. Perfect for a quick, affordable meal at lunchtime.

BRITISH

Boisdale
15 Eccleston St., SW1
⊖ Victoria
☎ 020 7730 6922
A winebar and restaurant combined, slightly odd in style, with an unusual and varied Franco-Scottish menu.

CHINESE

Hunan
51 Pimlico Rd, SW1
⊖ Victoria
☎ 020 7730 5712
This restaurant doesn't look much, but the food is always good. For those who like very spicy food.

Inn of Happiness
St Jame's Court Hotel
41-45 Buckingham Gate, SW1
⊖ Green Park
☎ 020 7821 1931
Nice atmosphere in this huge restaurant near Buckingham Palace.

MODERN EUROPEAN

Ebury Wine Bar and Restaurant
139 Ebury St., SW1
⊖ Sloane Square
☎ 020 7730 5447
The wine is sound and reliable while the food is inventive. A mixture of classic French or Italian, with a zest of modern.

BARS

Visitors to London the past had to do their drinking in traditional English pubs. Although these smoky, often dark and dingy watering-holes are still to be found on every London street, they are fast being replaced by trendy, continental-style bars serving a good selection of wines, wild cocktails and even coffee.
Here are a few for you to try.

Denim
4a St Martin's Lane, WC2
⊖ Leicester Square
☎ 020 7497 0376
For a delicious cocktail in a fashionable watering-hole, try Denim with its trendy seventies interior, beautiful clientele and funky music. The bar staff and bouncers are ultra cool and the drinks are expensive but the atmosphere is swish, upbeat and friendly and the plush red room downstairs is definitely worth a look.

Waxy O'Connors
14-16 Rupert St., W1
⊖ Piccadilly Circus
☎ 020 7287 0255
A hugely popular Irish-bar situated between Leicester Square and Piccadilly Circus. It has an impressive interior on many levels that spans an entire block below ground. Several bars and a restaurant, featuring ecclesiastical features imported from Ireland (including a large dead tree embedded into plaster at the podium level).

Gordons Wine Bar
47 Villiers St. WC2
⊖ Charing Cross
☎ 020 7930 1408
Claims to be the oldest drinking spot in town and is certainly one of the most curious. Dark, subterranean and magical, this

wine bar is perfect for sharing a bottle or two over the flickering candles. Look out for the wartime newspaper front pages on the walls.

Oxford Circus

The Social
5 Little Portland St. W1
⊖ Oxford Circus
☎ 020 7636 4992
Hang out in the comfy booths of the wood-panelled upstairs bar, or move downstairs for a stark, modern and decidedly louder affair. A jukebox, DJs and the trendy-but-friendly crowd ensure a fun night.

RESTAURANTS & BARS

NOTES